D0252007

4866 987152 5650 2900 3714
0 511 055548 02989 666 1948

APOCALYPSE!

APOCALYPSE!

A NEW LOOK AT THE BOOK OF REVELATION

DAVID C. COOPER

Pathway
PRESS

Library of Congress Catalog Card Number: 99-070183

ISBN: 087148-0433

DEDICATION

To my children,

David Paul and Charlsi,

my source of perpetual joy.

CONTENTS

FOREWORD

In a day when society is focusing on being touched by an angel and the media are presenting major productions dealing with all types of myths and legends about the afterlife, it is important to take a new look at the Book of Revelation.

In a refreshing and flowing style, Dr. David Cooper reminds each of us from all walks of life to stop and hear clearly what the Spirit is saying about God's future for the world and humanity.

For 25-plus years I have been closely associated with Pastor Cooper. As a teenager he was a part of the Mount Paran Church of God congregation in Atlanta, Georgia, where I served as senior pastor for 37 years. A close friend of my two sons, Paul Dana and Mark, he and Paul Dana (who was killed in an automobile accident in 1980) were college roommates and started their ministries together in the late 1970s.

After a period of evangelizing and serving in youth ministry, David and his wife, Barbie, utilized start-up help from Mount Paran to build a strong congregation of more than 1,000 people in Athens, Georgia.

During my last six years as senior pastor, David was called to serve as the associate pastor of Mount Paran Central—flagship congregation of the "one church in five locations" outreach of Mount Paran. When I was elected general overseer of the Church of God and accepted pastor emeritus status, Dr. Cooper was appointed senior pastor of Mount Paran Central in 1997. At the same time my son, Mark, was appointed senior pastor of Mount Paran North, the other flagship church of the Mount Paran ministries.

Through the years, my wife, Carmelita, and I have been blessed to be a part of the Cooper story of effective ministry and outreach for the kingdom of God.

From his background in evangelism, church planting, pastoring a megachurch and counseling, Dr. Cooper presents *Apocalypse!* as a practical guide to making the Revelation come alive in every aspect of living. In his words, "The Book of Revelation calls us heavenward" and urges us to find the "secret of true happiness and prosperity. . . ."

Dr. Cooper explains the events of the Apocalypse and illustrates them in a contemporary way that brings the reader to a face-to-face confrontation with the coming of Christ, who says, "I'm on my way! I'll be there soon!" In response we say, "Yes! Come, Master Jesus!" (Revelation 22:20, *TM*).

This book is for our times and I recommend it as a valuable resource for preaching, teaching and personal reading for ministers, church leaders, laypersons and especially the nonbelieving public.

Paul L. Walker, **Ph.D.**
General Overseer, Church of God
Pastor Emeritus,
Mount Paran Church of God, Atlanta, Ga.

INTRODUCTION

At the age of 45, Jack Wurm had reached the depths of depression and despair. Having failed in his business, he was walking on a California beach between job interviews.

As he strolled along the beach he noticed a half-hidden bottle in the sand. He stooped down to examine it. Seeing a note inside, he broke it open and read:

> To avoid confusion I leave my entire estate to the
> lucky person who finds this bottle and to my attorney,
> Barry Cohen, share and share alike. Daisy Alexander.
> June 20, 1937.

The name Daisy Alexander didn't mean anything to Jack Wurm, so he dismissed it as a joke. Later, however, he learned that Daisy Alexander was heiress to the vast Singer Sewing Machine fortune. If he could prove the validity of the note, he would be entitled to half of her $12 million estate.

Daisy Singer Alexander was an eccentric in England who often tossed bottles into the water to see where they would go. In 1939, she died at 82 and had left no final will. Wurm filed a claim for the fortune and the case began to wind its way through a long court process.

An oceanographer testified that a bottle dropped in the Thames River could indeed wash into the English Channel, be swept to the North Sea, through the Bering Straits into the North Pacific, and end up in California or Mexico. The journey would take about 12 years.

In actuality, it had taken 11 3/4 years. Jack Wurm was awarded the fortune. He had found a treasure in a bottle!

The Book of Revelation gives us a treasure, not in a bottle but in a Book! When we read it and take its message to heart, we discover a spiritual fortune that enriches our faith. Contrary to popular opinion, the Revelation was not written to frighten us, but rather to alleviate our anxieties about the future.

Since some tend to think of Revelation more in terms of the future than the present, it may seem strange to you that I have chosen the title, *Apocalypse!* Yet, when it was written toward the end of the first century, John the Apostle emphasized the immediacy of the events recorded, saying, "The time is soon."

I assure you that when first-century Christians pondered the signs, symbols and scenes of the Revelation, they found the words to be highly relevant to their times. Likewise, we will look at apocalypse now — not something just for the future.

Revelation records seven messages of Jesus to the church. He ends each with the challenge: "He who has ears let him hear what the Spirit is saying to the churches." The question is, What is the Spirit of God saying to *us* in the Revelation?

Some interpret the Revelation from a strictly historical view, suggesting that its contents describe only the persecution of the early church by the Roman Empire. For them, the message of the book is encrypted in the tombs of those who have gone before us.

Others correlate various historical developments throughout the church age with the symbols in the book based on highly conjectural references. Allusions to the rise of Islam, the Protestant Reformation, the Counter-Reformation, the French Revolution, World War I, and so forth have been identified in the book; so they have identified "beast" with such personalties as Nero, Muhammad, Adolph Hitler and others.

Finally, there are those who take a totally futuristic approach to the book. They seal up the vision until the appointed time of the end. Of course, by then it will be too late to reap the benefits of its contents. But why would God go to the trouble of giving the church such a wonderful book if it has no relevance to our times?

I want you to go with me on a journey through the Revelation. Listen to what the Spirit of God is saying to the church here and now. There is no doubt that the struggling people of the first-century church related heavily to the Revelation. It is equally clear that the book unveils God's fantastic future—the events that will occur when Christ returns.

The eternal and enduring theme of the Apocalypse is a triumphant message of faith to our times!

— *Dr. David C. Cooper,*

Senior Minister
Mount Paran Central Church of God

Chapter

1

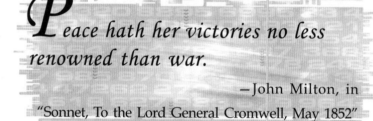

Peace hath her victories no less renowned than war.

—John Milton, in
"Sonnet, To the Lord General Cromwell, May 1852"

Peace

TAKE TO HEART
WHAT IS WRITTEN

*Blessed is the one who reads the words of this
prophecy, and blessed are those who hear it and
take to heart what is written in it, because the
time is near* (Revelation 1:3).

Get ready! When we read the Book of Revelation, we
step into a strange, unfamiliar world of angels
and demons, lambs and lions, horses and dragons.
Seals are broken. Trumpets blow. Seven bowls of wrath
pour out on the earth.

Two mysterious beasts emerge on the scene: the beast out
of the sea has 10 horns and seven heads, and the beast out
of the earth has lamb's horns and a dragon's voice.

The four horsemen of the apocalypse gallop onto the
stage of human history. We see 144,000 witnesses . . . the
sun-clothed woman and her manchild . . . the ancient

Serpent, called the devil or Satan . . . mystery Babylon the Great, mother of prostitutes and of the abominations of the earth.

From the throne of God comes thunder and lightning, hail and fire, earthquakes and plagues. Stars fall. The sky recedes like a scroll. The moon turns to blood. The sun turns black as sackcloth. Demon locusts are loosed from the Abyss. Men seek death but cannot find it. The earth is scorched. The seas and rivers turn to blood.

The armies of the world gather together for the final war at a place called Armageddon.

At first glance the Book of Revelation seems to be little more than a series of bizarre and meaningless visions written by an aged apostle. But when we read the opening verses we suddenly realize that the book contains a vital message for our times:

> The revelation of Jesus Christ, which God gave him to show his servants what must soon take place. He made it known by sending his angel to his servant John, who testifies to everything he saw — that is, the word of God and the testimony of Jesus Christ. Blessed is the one who reads the words of this prophecy, and blessed are those who hear it and take to heart what is written in it, because the time is near (Revelation 1:1-3).

People look at the Book of Revelation in different ways. Some view it as a book of confusion. They struggle to sort out the meaning of its symbolism and get lost in its imagery.

Others see it as a book of controversy. They like to debate different theological positions regarding the last days and assert their personal opinions with unabashed dogmatism. Still others view it as a book of consternation. They find themselves filled with fear and apprehension about the future when they read the Revelation. In reality, however, the Revelation was inspired by God, written by the apostle John and given to us as a book of peace to encourage and strengthen our faith. Let's take a close look at its message of peace.

Pay careful attention to the title of the book — *The Revelation*. It is a "revelation" not a "concealment." I point this out because many people think that the Revelation is full of deep, hidden secrets that we cannot comprehend. But the word *revelation*, or *apocalypse*, simply means to openly disclose and make known that which was previously hidden.

In the Revelation God pulls back the veil and shows us His eternal throne, power and glory as He works out His will for the world in the final chapter of history. This is why John says that the revealing was given "to show his servants (that's us) what must soon take place."

In a very real way the Revelation transports us into Heaven itself so that we can see everything that happens in human history — past, present, and future — from the vantage point of eternity.

The Book of Revelation gives to us an eternal perspective in a temporal world. This is by far its greatest blessing. It enables us to see such awe-inspiring scenes as the throne of God, Jesus Christ reigning triumphantly and returning in glory, and the Holy Spirit who is represented as "the seven spirits before the throne."

It also shows us the four living creatures, or cherubim, crying, "Holy, Holy, Holy," around God's throne; the raptured church in heaven; and countless multitudes around the throne, joyfully praising God. We are even shown the horrific works of the devil on earth and the final judgment of God against evil. In the Revelation, God reveals all things to us about both the natural world of man's inhumanity against man, and the supernatural realm of angels and demons. He leaves nothing uncovered.

Several important words and phrases in the opening statements put the book into its proper perspective.

Not only is it a revelation, it is a specific revelation — *the revelation of Jesus Christ.* Jesus, then, is the central figure of the drama. He is referred to as the Son of Man, the Lion of the tribe of Judah, the Root and the Offspring of David, the Lamb of God, and the King of kings and Lord of lords. This means that the Revelation is all about Him and His ministry as our Redeemer and Judge.

The phrases "what must soon take place" and "the time is near" leap off the page. They tell us that the contents of the book not only concern the distant future of the last days but also the condition of the times in which the book was written — the first century.

So the Revelation is more than a collection of secret clues about the future; it is a message for the people of God here and now. As John says, the time is near.

Finally, how can we overlook the word *blessed*? It means, "Oh, how happy." What a paradox: Oh, how happy are those who read and understand and take to heart the message of the horrors of the Revelation. This makes us want to read further to find out what wonderful message is contained in the book.

When you read "blessed. . . ." you think of the Beatitudes given by Jesus in His Sermon on the Mount in Matthew 5:3-10: Blessed are the poor in spirit. . . . Blessed are the merciful. . . . Blessed are the peacemakers. . . . and so forth.

But in the Revelation we find another series of His beatitudes that have been overlooked far too long. Altogether there are seven beatitudes given by Jesus in the Revelation:

✝ *Blessed is the one who reads the words of this prophecy, and blessed are those who hear it and take to heart what is written in it, because the time is near* (Revelation 1:3).

✝ *Then I heard a voice from heaven say, "Write: Blessed are the dead who die in the Lord from now on." "Yes," says the Spirit, "they will rest from their labor, for their deeds will follow them"* (14:13).

✝ *"Behold, I come like a thief! Blessed is he who stays awake and keeps his clothes with him, so that he may not go naked and be shamefully exposed"* (16:15).

✝ *Then the angel said to me, "Write: 'Blessed are those who are invited to the wedding supper of the Lamb!' And he added, "These are the true words of God"* (19:9).

✝ *"Blessed and holy are those who have part in the first resurrection. The second death has no power over them, but they will be priests of God and of Christ and will reign with him for a thousand years"* (20:6).

✝ *"Behold, I am coming soon! Blessed is he who keeps the words of the prophecy in this book"* (22:7).

✝ *"Blessed are those who wash their robes, that they may have the right to the tree of life and may go through the gates into the city"* (22:14).

These beatitudes give a positive message of hope about the future. So many people get uptight when they read the about the end of the world. It's like the story I heard about the end of the world.

God decided it was time to end the world, so He looked around and called together those whom He considered to be the three most influential men in the world at the time—Bill Clinton, Fidel Castro and Bill Gates. "I'm going to end the world," God told them. "You must go tell the people."

President Clinton made a live statement on all the major news networks: "I have good news and I have bad news," he said. "The good news is that we have been right all along—there *is* a God; the bad news is that He is ending the world."

Castro sent out a worldwide message to all Communists. "I have bad news and worse news," he said. "The bad news is that we have been wrong all along—there *is* a God. The worse news is that He is ending the world."

Bill Gates got on his computer and sent out a worldwide e-mail over the Internet. "I have good news and I have better news," he wrote. "The good news is that God thinks I'm one of the three most influential men in the world. The better news is we don't have to upgrade *Windows* anymore!"

Well, the Revelation contains good news for our times. To tap into its message of good news we must view the book as a three-fold revelation:

- ✝ A revelation to the church
- ✝ A revelation of Jesus Christ
- ✝ A revelation of the future.

A REVELATION
TO THE CHURCH

John the apostle was exiled to the island of Patmos by Emperor Domitian, the Roman ruler responsible for instituting emperor worship. Under the law of emperor worship, Roman citizens were required to pledge their

allegiance to the emperor by declaring, "Caesar is Lord!"
Christians refused, of course. Their declaration was, "Jesus
Christ is Lord." For that creed they lived, and for that creed
they died!

Patmos is a small, crescent-shaped, rocky island about 10
miles long and five miles wide. Located off the coast of
Turkey in the Aegean Sea, Patmos was a first-century penal
colony for hardened criminals.

John spent two years on Patmos before being released in
A.D. 96 by Nerva, who repealed the savage laws of emperor
worship. As an exile John represents the entire persecuted
and suffering church:

> *I, John, your brother and companion in the suffering and
> kingdom and patient endurance that are ours in Jesus, was on
> the island of Patmos because of the word of God and the
> testimony of Jesus (1:9).*

Spiritual Symbolism

Give careful attention to the words *suffering, kingdom* and
patient endurance. They describe a life of unshakable faith in
Christ regardless of the circumstances. John says he was
exiled "because of the word of God and the testimony of
Jesus." This phrase reappears throughout the Revelation to
describe the people of God who hold fast to their faith
despite personal pain or political persecution.

Today, believers all around the world are counting the
cost of their faith. More Christians have died in the 20th
century for the cause of Christ than at any other single
period of church history.

In some countries Christians are forbidden to gather for
public worship due to political restrictions of religious

freedom. For example, Christians can no longer worship in the American Consulate in Jidda, Saudi Arabia.

The country allows no places of worship other than Muslim mosques. Tim Hunter, who served at the consulate from 1993 to 1994, asked permission to worship in his own home but was denied that right.[1]

Countless other cases could be cited to document the persecution of Christians around the world—persecution that ranges from economic injustice to imprisonment and even death. Such upheaval characterized the age in which the Revelation was given to John.

At the turn of the first century the early church faced persecution from without by the Roman government and spiritual decline from within through the deception of false teachers. Jesus confronts these two enemies head-on in His messages to the seven churches in Asia Minor (Revelation 2:3).

The bottom line is that the Revelation was written to challenge and encourage God's people to hold on to their faith and remain faithful to their mission in the world. That's why we read such challenges as "This calls for patient endurance and faithfulness on the part of the saints" (13:10).

When we fail to see the central place the church plays in the unfolding drama of the Revelation we miss the point of the book altogether. The church is depicted through a series of symbols beginning with the seven golden lampstands among which Jesus stands (1:12, 13, 20).

The lampstands are reminiscent of the ones that provided light for the Holy Place in the Old Testament temple. It speaks of the church's role as "the light of the world" (Matthew 5:14).

The church is also portrayed as 24 elders (Revelation 4:4),

the 144,000 sealed with the seal of God (7:1-8; 14:1-4), those who had been victorious over the Beast and his image (15:2), the bride of Christ (19:7; 21:9), and the New Jerusalem (21:2).

Notice the multiples of 12 in the symbols which derive from the 12 tribes of Israel and the 12 apostles of Christ. The people of God are both Old and New Testament believers and worshipers of the living God.

While the letter was originally sent to seven literal churches in Asia Minor (modern Turkey), these seven churches also represent the entire body of Christ throughout Christian history.   The number seven stands for completeness or perfection.

Further, the Book of Revelation unravels the mystery of the spiritual conflict that exists between the present world system and the church. This ongoing conflict is motivated by the powers of evil under the direction of Satan himself as he wars against the people of God.

The Revelation sheds light on what we refer to today as spiritual warfare.

Seven Seals

John sees a vision of a seven-sealed scroll which Jesus takes from the hand of God. The Lord proceeds to open its seals and, thereby reveal its content (6:1). The seven-sealed scroll provides a panoramic view of church history and depicts the spiritual conflict between the church and the world. These seals also portray chaotic world conditions, or "signs of the times," that exist throughout the entire church age.

Each sign mounts in intensity until Christ returns in power and great glory to establish the kingdom of God on earth (see Matthew 24:1-35).

The famed four horsemen of the Apocalypse ride on the scene as the first four seals are opened.

First, there is *the white horse rider*, which is the Antichrist as well as the spirit of antichrist that is already at work in the world.

Then comes the *red horse rider* symbolic of wars, civil strife, martyrdom, and violence.

Third, the *black horse rider* gallops on the scene representing famine, economic injustice, poverty and starvation of global proportions.

He is followed by the *pale horse rider* called Death, and Hell followed him. What a terrifying scene ensues: "They were given power over a fourth of the earth to kill by sword, famine and plague, and by the wild beasts of the earth" (6:8).

As the fifth seal is opened (6:9-11), John sees the martyrs under the altar. He pays special attention to the fact that they had been slain "because of the word of God and the testimony they had maintained."

Also, "they called out in a loud voice, 'How long, Sovereign Lord, holy and true, until you judge the inhabitants of the earth and avenge our blood?' "

The martyrs were told to wait a little longer until the number of saints had been completed, that is, until the church age ends. Their cry for justice is a central theme in the book.

The answer to the cries come from the throne of God when John hears the heavenly announcement: "The kingdom of the world has become the kingdom of our Lord and of his Christ, and he will reign for ever and ever" (11:15). When the final chapter of human history plays out, God will redeem every injustice that has ever been committed.

The sixth seal gives us a preview of the coming judgment of God. The Biblical concept of judgment includes both the direct action of God and the natural consequences of sin. Let's be honest about it, most of the judgment we face is merely the result of the consequences of our sins. As Paul said, we reap what we sow (Galatians 6:7).

Such is the nature of many of the calamities depicted in Revelation. We bring on ourselves such catastrophes as war, famine, poverty, crime and political unrest.

This is why the sixth seal describes the heavens and the earth in a state of upheaval. This cosmic upheaval intensifies in the next two series of judgments recorded in the Revelation: the seven trumpets (chs 8-11) and the seven bowls of wrath, which complete God's judgment (chs 15, 16).

Eventually, the chaotic conditions of society will usher the world into a time of great tribulation under the global tyranny of the Antichrist. These apocalyptic signs are already appearing on the landscape of history. Listen to startling predictions by Robert D. Kaplan, in his article titled "The Coming Anarchy:"

> Nations break up under the tidal flow of refugees from environmental and social disaster. As borders crumble, another type of boundary is erected — a wall of disease. Wars are fought over scarce resources, especially water, and war itself becomes continuous with crime, as armed bands of stateless marauders clash with the private security forces of the elite. A preview of the first decades of the twenty-first century.[2]

Heavenly Silence

This series of the seven seals ends with a time of silence in heaven (8:1). Silence represents God's long-suffering, patience and mercy as He waits for humanity to repent and turn to Him for salvation and abundant life. Please know that God never delights in sending judgment.

Hosea tells us that God desires mercy not sacrifice (Hosea 6:6). When the prophet Joel saw the vision of the Armageddon, he reassured us that God is "gracious and compassionate, slow to anger and abounding in love, and he relents from sending calamity" (Joel 2:13).

The apostle Peter clarifies the meaning of the peaceful silence in heaven when he writes, "The Lord is not slow in keeping his promise, as some understand slowness. He is patient with you, not wanting anyone to perish, but everyone to come to repentance" (2 Peter 3:9).

God waits in patience during this time of heavenly silence, this day of grace, for everyone to come to Him.

Before going any further, let's review what we've learned up to this point:

✝ The purpose of the seven seals is to encourage the church to fulfill her mission even in the face of severe world conditions and political persecution.

✝ The Revelation underscores the fact that such conditions exist because the church is engaged in a great spiritual war.

This lets us know that chaotic world conditions are often the result of spiritual forces of evil at work behind the scenes moving, as it were, political leaders as pawns on the chessboard of history. John goes on to tell us that:

> Spirits of demons . . . go out to the kings of the whole world, to gather them for the battle of the great day of God Almighty. . . . to the place that in Hebrew is called Armageddon (16:14, 16).

Think of it: Demon spirits even drive nations to war against each other! I'm confident that that's what happened during World War II when Adolph Hitler tried to conquer the world . . . and again when Saddam Hussein invaded Kuwait and mercilessly slaughtered the people.

Make no mistake about it, spiritual warfare is real. You and I face it every day. This is why John reveals five spiritual enemies that we constantly face. They threaten to destroy both Israel and the church, which together make up the people of God. Who are these enemies?

1. The "beast out of the sea," the Antichrist to come as well as the spirit of antichrist already at work in the world (13:1-10)

2. The "beast out of the earth" or the False Prophet (13:11-15)

3. The mark of the Beast, 666, which represents economic persecution (13:16-18)

4. Mystery Babylon the Great, the force of spiritual and political persecution and martyrdom (14:8; 16:19; 17:1-18:24)

5. The Great Red Dragon (also called the Ancient Serpent), Satan himself, who leads the whole world astray (12:3-12)

These are our real enemies today as well as in the future. Now for the good news. Not only does John see the church in conflict with these forces, but more importantly, he declares that we are more than conquerors over our enemies.

The victorious church is portrayed in John's vision of the seven lampstands, which continue to shine forth the light of the gospel of Christ in spite of opposition and persecution.

The Bible says the light shines in the darkness, and the darkness has not conquered it (see John 1:5).

We also hear the theme of victory every time we read the phrase "To him who overcomes." The primary purpose of Revelation is to affirm the great promise of Jesus to His church as it faces spiritual warfare: "Upon this rock I will build my church; and the gates of hell shall not prevail against it" (Matthew 16:18, *KJV*). This is the real message of Revelation.

A REVELATION OF
JESUS CHRIST

How did John come to receive such a magnificent and awe-inspiring series of visions which have intrigued those who have read it for nearly 2,000 years? Jesus paid John a personal visit while he was in exile. Jesus appeared in such glory that John searched for words to describe His majesty:

> *On the Lord's Day I was in the Spirit, and I heard behind me a loud voice like a trumpet. . . .*
>
> *I turned around to see the voice that was speaking to me. And when I turned I saw seven golden lampstands, and among the lampstands was someone "like a son of man," dressed in a robe reaching down to his feet and with a golden sash around his chest. His head and hair were white like wool, as white as snow, and his eyes were like blazing fire. His feet were like bronze glowing in a furnace, pand his voice was like the sound of rushing waters. In his right hand he held seven stars, and out of his mouth came a sharp double-edged sword. His face was like the sun shining in all its brilliance (1:10, 12-16).*

Jesus Christ is the central figure of the unfolding drama. John gives Him the title "son of man." The Son of Man is an

Old Testament messianic title based on Daniel's vision of the second coming of Christ:

> *In my vision at night I looked, and there before me was one like a son of man, coming with the clouds of heaven. He approached the Ancient of Days and was led into his presence. He was given authority, glory and sovereign power; all peoples, nations and men of every language worshiped him. His dominion is an everlasting dominion that will not pass away, and his kingdom is one that will never be destroyed* (Daniel 7:13, 14).

During His earthly ministry, Jesus' favorite title of self-designation was this title, the Son of Man. It appears 86 times in the Gospels.

In the opening vision, John hears the voice of the Son of Man speaking to him like a trumpet. The analogy of the loud trumpet brings to mind the experience of Moses, who heard the voice of God thundering like a trumpet on Mount Sinai. The trumpet blast signifies the awesome power and holy authority of God's eternal, omnipotent Word.

THE RISEN
LORD

In the beginning, God spoke and the heavens and earth were formed. With that same power, Jesus, the One who has all authority in heaven and earth (Matthew 28:18), speaks to the church.

The fact that Jesus speaks in the vision tells us that we serve a living Savior who speaks to His people through the presence of the Holy Spirit. Jesus sends a divine letter, or epistle, to each of the seven churches of Asia Minor. They teach timeless truths to all believers who will hear and receive them. Each message ends with Christ's saying, "He who has an ear let him hear what the Spirit says to the churches."

Chapters 2 and 3 of Revelation challenge us to listen carefully to what Christ is saying in these messages. Not only is the voice of Jesus awe-inspiring, sounding like a majestic trumpet blast, but His dazzling appearance is so overwhelming that John falls at His feet as though dead.

A closer look at this glorious appearance of our Lord is certainly in order. The fact that Jesus is amid the lampstands assures us that in the midst of trials and tribulations God will accomplish His purpose, historically and personally, and will bring us forth triumphant and refined as pure gold.

But He doesn't appear on the island of Patmos as He appeared in Bethlehem's manger, as the Christ of the Beatitudes, or even as the crucified Savior. Rather, He appears in the fullness of His glory as the resurrected, triumphant Lamb of God (see 1:13-16).

He is dressed in a robe that reaches to His feet; it has a golden sash which encircles His chest. The priestly garment of Jesus, our great High Priest who ever lives to make intercession for the world, is a golden sash depicting His royalty as king.

His head and hair are white like wool, as white as snow. This description ascribes to Christ the patriarchal dignity of One who is co-equal, co-existent and co-eternal, with God the Father.

His eyes are like blazing fire. The flames of fire call to attention to His holiness and truth which search our hearts and minds. He knows the thoughts and the intents of our hearts.

His feet are like bronze glowing in a furnace. Bronze was heavily used in the construction of Moses's tabernacle and represents God's judgment against sin.

Jesus was judged for the sins of the world on the cross so that the whole world might be forgiven. And in the last days He will return with feet of bronze to crush the kingdom of the Antichrist and to establish His eternal kingdom.

His voice is like the sound of rushing waters. When Jesus spoke, demons were cast out, sicknesses were healed, the loaves and fish were multiplied, the winds and waves became still, and the dead came to life.

In His right hand He holds seven stars. Jesus holds His people (represented by the seven stars) in His right hand, providing providential care and security. He promises, "No one can snatch them out of my hand" (John 10:28).

Out of his mouth goes a sharp double-edged sword. With His word He spoke the worlds into existence; and He will come again with His Word to destroy all that is evil.

His face is like the sun shining in all its brilliance. He radiates the glory of God . . . the same glory Moses saw at Mount Sinai . . . the same glory His disciples saw on the Mount of Tranfiguration . . . and the same glory Saul of Tarsus saw on the Damascus road. When John saw the New Jerusalem, where believers will spend eternity, he said, "The city does not need the sun or the moon to shine on it, for the glory of God gives it light, and the Lamb is its lamp" (21:23).

Fear Not!

John is so overwhelmed by this extra-terrestrial visitation of the Son of Man that he tells us, "When I saw him, I fell at his feet as though dead." Wouldn't you?

Then he placed his right hand on me and said: "Do not be afraid. I am the First and the Last. I am the Living One; I was dead, and behold I am alive for ever and ever! And I hold the keys of death and Hades" (1:17, 18).

You see, the awesome power of God is the power of His love and mercy. The act of Jesus touching John is so descriptive of the way Christ touches us at the point of our fears and anxieties, and whispers in our hearts, "Fear not!"

Did you know that the simple message "Fear not!" appears more than 80 times in the Bible? God reassures us constantly of His presence, power and providential care. This was Jesus' message to John on Patmos that day.

When we understand the visitation of Christ we realize that the primary purpose of the Revelation is not to instill fear but rather to dispel fear. This book is a book of peace. What peace is ours when we hear the message of the Lord of the church.

✝ When the seven seals are opened—*fear not!*

✝ When the seven trumpet judgments blast with divine fury—*fear not!*

✝ When the seven bowls of wrath are poured out on the earth—*fear not!*

✝ When the Antichrist rises to power—*fear not!*

✝ When the False Prophet deceives the nations—*fear not!*

✝ When the mark of the Beast is enforced—*fear not!*

✝ When Mystery Babylon the Great martyrs the righteous—*fear not!*

✝ When the Dragon seeks to destroy the saints—*fear not!*

Fear Not . . . Why Not?

Why should we not be afraid of the horribly terrifying judgments coming on the world? Why shouldn't we be afraid of the rise of the Antichrist and the certainty of the Armageddon? Jesus gives us three reasons we should not fear:

1. *Fear not, for I am the First and the Last.* Jesus is the beginning of creation and the ultimate goal of history. The purpose of God is stated clearly by the apostle Paul:

> *And he made known to us the mystery of his will according to his good pleasure, which he purposed in Christ, to be put into effect when the times will have reached their fulfillment – to bring all things in heaven and on earth together under one head, even Christ* (Ephesians 1:9, 10).

History is linear, spinning out of control, repeating itself in meaningless cycles. It begins with creation in Genesis; and is completed with a new creation in Revelation. What God started in Genesis, He completes in Revelation.

✝ In Genesis, Satan became the god of this world; in Revelation, Satan is destroyed in the lake of fire.

✝ In Genesis, man was separated from God by sin; in Revelation, man is reconciled to God in the New Jerusalem.

✝ In Genesis, sin brought the curse; in the Revelation there will be no more curse.

✝ In Genesis, death and hell came into existence; in Revelation, death and hell are destroyed.

✝ In Genesis, the gates of paradise (Garden of Eden) are closed; in Revelation, paradise (heaven) is opened and we have the right to eat from the Tree of Life.

✝. In Genesis, suffering, sorrow and death became part of the human experience; in Revelation there will be no more death, pain or sorrow.

✝ In Genesis, man lost his inheritance; in Revelation, man will inherit all things.

2. Fear not, for I am the Living One. All early extra-Biblical sources agree that three days after Jesus was buried in it, His tomb was empty. Even the Roman government testified of the empty tomb after the Roman seal on the tomb was broken and the guards were terrified by an angelic visitation.

The resurrection of Jesus is the foundation of our faith today and our hope for tomorrow. As C. S. Lewis observed: "The first fact in the history of Christendom is the number of people who say they have seen the resurrected Christ. If they had died without making anyone else believe this 'gospel,' no Gospels would have ever been written."

Abraham, the father of Judaism, lived 19 centuries before Christ—he has not risen.Buddha lived five centuries before Christ and died at age 80—he has not risen. Muhammad lived six centuries after Christ and died in A.D. 632—he has not risen.

But when we visit the tomb of Jesus in Jerusalem, the angelic announcement of hope can still be heard: "Why do you look for the living among the dead? He is not here; he has risen!"(Luke 24:5, 6).

3. Fear not, I hold the keys of death and hell. The keys represent Christ's power and authority. This statement means that Jesus is in complete control of everything that happens in this world, and even in our own personal lives.

At His ascension He declared, "All authority in heaven and on earth has been given to me. Therefore, go and make disciples of all nations" (Matthew 28:18, 19). The church is commissioned to minister in the full power and authority of the risen Lord.

This is why, even in the face of emperor worship, first century Christians refused to confess, "Caesar is Lord." He wasn't lord of anything or anybody. Instead, they declared boldly, "Jesus Christ is Lord!"

We don't *make* Jesus Lord; He *is* Lord! It is a misnomer for modern Christians to speak of making Jesus Lord.

Paul the apostle said:

> *Therefore God exalted him to the highest place and gave him the name that is above every name, that at the name of Jesus every knee should bow, in heaven and on earth and under the earth, and every tongue confess that Jesus Christ is Lord, to the glory of God the Father* (Philippians 2:9-11).

What does Christ's lordship mean in your life? Maybe this story will help answer the question for you.

Johann Dannecker, the German sculptor, worked for two years on a statue of Christ. After its completion he showed his work to a young girl who was at his studio and asked, "Who is that?"

She pondered the figure but had to admit that she wasn't sure who it was. Dannecker knew he had failed to capture the compelling love of Christ in his art.

He then worked on a second statue for six years. During that time he said Jesus appeared to him. Later, he said that he merely transferred to the marble the vision he had seen. The result was a stunning sculpture of Jesus Christ.

Sometime later Napoleon requested Dannecker to make a statue of Venus for the Louvre, but he refused.

"A man who has seen the Christ," he said, "can never use his gifts to carve the image of a pagan goddess. My art is henceforth a consecrated thing."

A REVELATION OF
THE FUTURE

Are you understanding the impact of this wonderful book? Over and over in the Revelation the people of God are assured that the final outcome of history rests solely in the hands of an omnipotent, merciful God.

There is no doubt that the Revelation is our guide to the future. John was given the following instructions:

> Write, therefore, what you have seen, what is now and what will take place later. The mystery of the seven stars that you saw in my right hand and of the seven golden lampstands is this: The seven stars are the angels of the seven churches, and the seven lampstands are the seven churches (1:19, 20).

Disclosing the Judgment of God

As we look into the future through the eyes of the Revelator, we see both judgment and reward. Every person will ultimately face either judgment or reward in eternity.

The sure judgment of a loving God is depicted first in the sixth seal:

> I watched as he opened the sixth seal. There was a great earthquake. The sun turned black like sackcloth made of goat hair, the whole moon turned blood red, and the stars in the sky fell to earth, as late figs drop from a fig tree when shaken by a strong wind. The sky receded like a scroll, rolling up, and every mountain and island was removed from its place.
>
> Then the kings of the earth, the princes, the generals, the rich, the mighty, and every slave and every free man hid in caves and among the rocks of the mountains. They called to the mountains and the rocks, "Fall on us and hide us from the face of him who sits on the throne and from the wrath of the Lamb! For the great day of their wrath has come, and who can stand?" (6:12-17).

Revealing the Rewards of the Faithful

After this terrifying scene unfolds we catch our first glimpse of the eternal reward we will share with Christ. John tells us in no uncertain terms:

> After this I looked and there before me was a great multitude that no one could count, from every nation, tribe, people and language, standing before the throne and in front of the Lamb. They were wearing white robes and were holding palm branches in their hands. And they cried out in a loud voice: "Salvation belongs to our God, who sits on the throne, and to the Lamb."

> [One of the elders said,] "They are before the throne of God and serve him day and night in his temple; and he who sits on the throne will spread his tent over them. Never again will they hunger; never again will they thirst. The sun will not beat upon them, nor any scorching heat. For the Lamb at the center of the throne will be their shepherd; he will lead them to springs of living water. And God will wipe away every tear from their eyes" (7:9, 10, 15-17).

Discerning the Signs of the Times

While it is easy to become alarmed by world conditions, we need to look for signs of hope on the horizon. If the Revelation gives us any gift for life, it gives us the gift of hope for our times.

One of the most positive signs of the times is the explosive world-wide response to the gospel. According to the article "A Christian World By 2000?" research indicates that some 1,200 plans by Christian organizations exist which have as their goal to evangelize the globe by the year 2000.

Other plans focus on specific geographical areas. Christians now comprise at least a third of the world's 5.9 billion population.

Right now, however, it is estimated that about 1.7 billion people have no access to the Christian gospel.[3] However, every possible effort is being made to make sure they hear the gospel of Christ.

This information is exciting in light of Jesus' prophecy concerning the last days:

> "And this gospel of the kingdom will be preached in the whole world as a testimony to all nations, and then the end will come" (Matthew 24:14).

I meet many people today who have a deep interest in the future and, in particular, the return of Christ. No doubt, this renewed interest in Bible prophecy is linked to the hype surrounding the arrival of a new millennium.

Over the past few years I have had the privilege of sharing my faith with a gentleman who is an orthodox Jew. He has been very interested in learning more about Jesus for some time now.

One day he said to me, "I have been reading the New Testament, and I now believe in Jesus. I know that he is the Son of God."

We talked for a while about how Jesus fulfilled the messianic prophecies of the Old Testament. Then he asked me,"When you look at world conditions, do you think His coming is near?"

I told him, "I don't know. Jesus said, 'No one knows the day nor the hour.' But, one thing is for sure, He will come one day." This folk song is from the era of the Civil War. I think it captures best the hope we have in our Lord's return:

There's a King and Captain high,
    And He's coming by and by,
And He'll find me hoeing cotton when He comes.

Peace: Take To Heart What Is Written

You can hear His legions charging
    in the regions of the sky,
And He'll find me hoeing cotton when He comes.

There's a Man they thrust aside,
    Who was tortured till He died,
And He'll find me hoeing cotton when He comes.

He was hated and rejected,
    He was scorned and crucified,
And He'll find me hoeing cotton when He comes.

When He comes! When He comes!
He'll be crowned by saints and angels when He comes.
They'll be shouting out "Hosanna!"
    to the Man that men denied,
And I'll kneel among my cotton when He comes.

— Author unknown

Chapter
2

Scatter, as from an unextinguished hearth
Ashes and sparks, my words among mankind!
Be through my lips to unawakened earth
The trumpet of a prophecy!

—Percy Bysshe Shelley in "Ozymandias"

THINGS TO COME

*Write, therefore, what you have seen,
what is now and what will take place
later* (Revelation 1:19).

The nuclear devastation of Hiroshima and Nagasaki had ended World War II when a war correspondent went on the radio from one of those cities, introduced himself with these words, "I am standing on the spot where the end of the world began."

Everyone is curious and concerned about the future. Where is our world heading? Nuclear holocaust? Global warming? Scarcity of resources? Or better, a new world order under a world-wide government? A utopian paradise created by humanistic technology? Some people turn to astrology, or to psychic prediction or to self-proclaimed prophets in their attempts to know the future.

Many look toward the year 2000 with great alarm. According to computer scientists and financial analysts, Y2K poses serious problems to the economy on a global scale. The U.S. Government's General Accounting Office says, "The public faces a high risk that critical services provided by the government and the private sector could be severely disrupted by the year 2000 computer crisis. Financial transactions could be delayed, flights grounded, power lost and national defense affected."

Y2K also "has the potential of disrupting communications services worldwide," says Federal Communications Commission chairman William Kennard in a report to the U.S. Senate. "The communications infrastructure is absolutely critical," he pointed out, "not only to the economy . . . but also to national preparedness, military, public safety, emergency and personal communications."[1]

Hopefully, the Y2K threat will serve as a catalyst to awaken people spiritually and turn them to Jesus Christ, the only hope for our world.

In these alarming times the Bible assures us that the future belongs to God, and it is glorious beyond words. The most prophetic book in the Bible is the Book of Revelation. The word "revelation" (Greek, *apokalupsis*) means "to uncover, to openly disclose or to make known that which was previously hidden." We get *apocalypse* from this word. This Revelation, this book, is an index to God's fantastic future.

Now the Revelation doesn't reveal everything that will be in the future. When considering the future we need to remember the counsel of Moses: "The secret things belong to the Lord our God, but the things revealed belong to us and to our children forever, that we may follow all the words of this law" (Deuteronomy 29:29).

Unfortunately, some scholars and teachers have erred in their attempts to read too much into apocalyptic symbolism in a futile effort to know it all. While we must honestly admit that no one knows everything about the future, the Revelation certainly pulls back the curtain to show us things to come.

SORTING OUT
THE SYMBOLS

Without a doubt, the Revelation makes the greatest use of apocalyptic symbolism found anywhere in the Bible. J. Daryl Charles points out:

> The force of symbolic language lies in its ability to super-
> sede human categories. . . . The theology of John is visual
> theology; seeing is understanding. The audience will
> experience earthquakes, storms, fire, pain, joy, worship,
> agony and delirium . . . to encourage Christians to an
> active, not passive, participation in history.[2]

Several points need to be made about the symbolism and numerology in order to really grasp the message of the Revelation.

First, the symbolism and numerology is rooted in the Old Testament, and in particular the apocalyptic writings of the Pentateuch and the Prophets. This means that the symbols and numbers remain consistent throughout Scripture. Bear in mind that the numbers employed—such as 7, 10, 12 and so forth, seldom, if ever, represent numerical values. Instead, they represent spiritual concepts or principles.

Seven stands for perfection or completeness. *Twelve* is the number of divine government and the people of God, as typified in the 12 tribes of Israel and the 12 apostles of Christ. This includes multiples of 12, such as 24 and 144,000. The number of man, who is less than perfect or divine, is **666**. It obviously represents man in rebellion to God.

Forty is the number of divine testing of the Israelites. It is the number of years Israel spent in the wilderness. It represents preparation in the case of Moses being in the mountain for 40 days. It represents both testing and preparation in the number of days Jesus underwent testing in His temptation.

Three is the number of the Trinity. *Four* is the number that represents all creation. Examples are the references to the four winds of heaven and the four corners of the earth (see 7:1). More will be said about these numbers as we move further into our study in later chapters.

Second, be consistent when interpreting the symbols from scene to scene as the drama unfolds. This means if the number 7 is considered symbolic in chapter 1, then it needs to be considered symbolic in later chapters as well. Great confusion and misunderstanding occurs when the symbols are interpreted inconsistently and the meanings shift back and forth from literal to symbolic.

Third, the meaning of each symbol must be taken as a whole. Avoid picking the symbols apart by trying to give specific meaning to each detail. Each symbol, then, such as the throne of God or the seven seals, is intended to paint a mental picture of a spiritual or historical reality.

Every intricate detail of the symbols is not designed to carry a specific meaning. One can easily infer more from these symbolic visions than is warranted or intended. Great error has occurred over the years by futile efforts to unlock secrets about future events, such as the identity of the

Antichrist, the designation of the nations in his empire, or even the timing of Jesus' second coming.

Fourth, two types of symbols are used: those representing specific historical events and those representing spiritual truths. Sometimes a symbol carries a double meaning, as in the case of the seven churches in Asia Minor to whom the book was originally sent (1:10, 11). While these churches actually existed (the remains of most can still be visited today in Turkey), they also represent the complete church down through the ages.

Fifth, seven is the most frequently used number in the Revelation. The number seven means completion, fulfillment or perfection. It is used 54 times to represent God's completion of His redemptive plan for humanity. This is the plan He works out in history.

The various series of seven, such as the seals, trumpets, bowls, lampstands, churches and so forth, provide descriptions of principles of human conduct and divine government currently at work in the world. The Revelation, then, deals simultaneously with the present and the future.

Sixth, the most frequently used symbol in the Revelation is the throne of God. John speaks of the throne 45 times to represent the sovereignty of God. The throne underscores the main purpose of the Revelation—namely, to encourage believers to recognize that God rules over all.

I want to state emphatically that the Revelation is no way intended to provide futuristic clues for the curious. On the contrary, the visions enable us to evaluate world events from the vantage point of the sovereign God who is seated on His heavenly throne.

Whatever trials, tribulations or persecution we may face, the message of the Revelation affirms Romans 8:37: "In all these things we are more than conquerors through him who loved us."

Seventh, always adopt the meaning of the symbols which is most obviously consistent with the remainder of Scripture. Avoid looking for more secretive, hidden meanings. Remember, the purpose of the Revelation is to make known what God is doing in the world, not to hide it.

You don't have to look for hidden meanings. They aren't there. The message is openly revealed and easy to understand if you don't try to read more into the symbolism than God intended.

CONCEPTUAL OR CHRONOLOGICAL?

Now that we have a handle on the symbolism, we need to deal with another important feature of the Revelation: namely, the fact that the visions do not form a continuous line of chronological history.

Confusion results when one tries to impose on the book a strict timeline from chapter 1 through chapter 22. Instead of a pure chronology, John plays the same themes over and over, each time using greater detail and intensity, much like a musical score for an opera.

Scenes of judgment and wrath are often repeated, as well as scenes of victory and reward. For example, the new heaven and new earth are introduced first in chapter 7, but fully revealed much later in chapter 21.

✝ In the same way, the Battle of Armageddon is mentioned first of all when the sixth seal is opened (6:12-17).

✝ It is cited again in the sounding of the sixth trumpet judgment (9:13-16; 14:14-20).

✝ A third time Armageddon is mentioned in the account of the sixth bowl of wrath (16:16).

✝ Finally, we read of the Battle of Armageddon at the return of Christ (19:11-21).

You can see how the theme of Armageddon is presented in repetitive fashion as the image builds in intensity each time it appears. By the way, did you catch the three series of six, 666, just mentioned? Interesting isn't it?

Here's the point. A general chronology of the future exists in the Revelation involving great apocalyptic signs such as the Great Tribulation period, the second coming of Christ, the final judgment and eternity with God.

But the series of visions are intended to show us the unfolding drama of church history, not to give us a strict chronology of everything that will happen in the future. Having laid this important groundwork, we are ready to take a journey together into the future according to faith.

NOW FOR
THE MAIN EVENT

It is interesting to note that while the Old Testament contains 300 prophecies concerning the first coming of the Messiah, the New Testament has 318 prophecies of His return. In fact, one out of every 25 verses in the New Testament assures us that Jesus will come to earth again.

Christ's return is the main event of the future. A *U.S. News & World Report* poll reports that 61 percent of Americans believe in the second coming of Christ.[3]

This event, the return of Christ, will take place in two phases. First, He will come to rapture His church out of the earth and then, at the end of the age, He will come to establish the kingdom of God on earth. The Rapture is first.

The word *Rapture* comes from the Latin *rapio*, which means "to catch away suddenly." While the word *rapture* does not actually appear in the Bible, the concept certainly does.

✝ Paul writes eloquently: "For the Lord himself will come down from heaven, with a loud command, with the voice of the archangel and with the trumpet call of God, and the dead in Christ will rise first. After that, we who are still alive and are left will be *caught up together* with them in the clouds to meet the Lord in the air. And so we will be with the Lord forever. Therefore encourage each other with these words" (1 Thessalonians 4:16-18, *emphasis added*).

✝ Paul described this catching away as occurring "in a flash, in the twinkling of an eye" (1 Corinthians 15:51).

✝ Jesus told His disciples, "In my Father's house are many mansions: if it were not so, I would have told you. I go to prepare a place for you. And if I go and prepare a place for you, I will come again, and receive you unto myself; that where I am, there ye may be also" (John 14:2, 3, *KJV*).

✝ Paul also wrote, "Concerning the coming of our Lord Jesus Christ and our being gathered to him, we ask you, brothers, not to become easily unsettled" (2 Thessalonians 2:1, 2).

These verses paint a mental picture of the rapture of the church with the use of such phrases as "caught up," "to meet the Lord in the air," "receive you unto myself," "in the twinkling of an eye," and "our being gathered to him." Such terminology is quite distinct from other prophetic passages concerning the second phase of the coming of Christ.

The apostle John describes this second phase: "Look, he is coming with the clouds, and every eye will see him, even those who pierced him; and all the peoples of the earth will mourn because of him" (Revelation 1:7).

The Revelation further describes the return of Christ at the end of the Great Tribulation and the Battle of Armageddon. When He comes He is crowned as King of kings and Lord of lords, has a sharp sword proceeding from his mouth to strike down the nations, and He is treading the winepress of the fury and wrath of God Almighty (19:11-16).

The rapture of the church, then, is to be distinguished from the second coming of Christ. These are the two aspects of His return. Why is the Rapture important? For believers it will mean that they will:

✝ Receive their glorified bodies (Romans 8:18-25; Philippians 3:20, 21)

✝ Obtain their rewards at the judgment seat of Christ (Romans 14:10-12; 1 Corinthians 3:12–15; 2 Corinthians 5:10; 2 Timothy 4:8; Revelation 22:12)

✝ Celebrate the Marriage Supper of the Lamb in heaven (Revelation 19:6-9)

✝ Prepare for the second coming of Christ at the end of the Great Tribulation (19:11-16)

✝ Permit the rise of the Antichrist (2 Thessalonians 2:1-3).

Some scholars believe that both the Rapture and the second coming of Christ at the end of the Great Tribulation are the same event.

In all honesty it must be pointed out that one of the problems that faces all rapture theories is the fact that each perspective is based on inferences made from Scripture rather than explicit statements.

John Walvoord points out this problem by stating, "While both pretribulationists and post-tribulationists have strained to find some specific reference in support of their views, most adherents of either view usually concede that there is not explicit reference."[4]

Unfortunately, the subject of the Rapture has become a topic of debate and dissension in recent years. The tragedy of such divisiveness cannot be overstated.

I agree that one's position on the Rapture should never be used as a litmus test of faith. Christ's promise to return was not given by our Lord to be a source of theological division, but rather a source of eternal hope. We need to pause and ask, What did the early church believe about the return of Christ?

While early Christians did not have an elaborately developed theology of the last days, they held firmly to the truth of the imminent return of Christ. This means they believed that Jesus could return at any time. For them, the Day of the Lord was always at hand.

John Walvoord points out, "The early church lived in constant expectation of the coming of the Lord for His church.' "[5] Today, Christians need to live with the same level of expectant faith and joyful hope.

Instead of getting bogged down in theological debate, we need to be looking "for the blessed hope—the glorious appearing of our great God and Savior, Jesus Christ" (Titus 2:13).

SENSE AND
SENSIBILITY

We can learn some important lessons from our spiritual forefathers on this issue. The early church did not look for intervening signs or preparatory factors which had to be fulfilled before Jesus could return.

The Book of Revelation itself sets forth the imminency of His return in the opening phrase, "the time is near" (1:3). It closes with the personal promise of Christ, "Behold, I am coming soon!" (22:12). The expectation of the church is embodied in the words of John in response to Christ's promise of His return, "Amen. Come, Lord Jesus" (22:20).

This means that no prophecies have to be fulfilled before Christ returns for His church. The doctrine of imminency calls the people to a constant state of "ready alert." Jesus cautioned, "No one knows about that day or hour. . . . Therefore keep watch, because you do not know on what day your Lord will come" (Matthew 24:36, 42).

A travesty to Biblical prophecy occurs when people try to predict the timing of Christ's return. Years ago the Jehovah's Witnesses perpetuated the belief that the generation alive during World War I would witness the return of Christ. Other similar predictions have been made on other occasions by various pseudo-Christian groups in the name of prophecy.

In this same spirit of sensationalism, Edgar Whisenant of Arkansas and his followers distributed more than 2 million copies of his booklet, *88 Reasons Why The Rapture Will be in 1988*. When 1988 passed he wrote a new book explaining his miscalculations and stating that there was a 50 percent chance that Christ would return in 1989.

When the year passed, he said a bulk of Scripture pointed to 1992. After that theory proved false, callers dialing his toll-free telephone number got a promotional recording for a chiropractor.

An owner of a chain of Christian radio stations proclaimed in his broadcasts and in two books that the universe would come to an abrupt end between September 15 and 29 of 1994. Even a well-known Evangelical writer said recently that he did not expect to be around for the New Year's celebration that brings in the year 2000.

Such predictions reflect the height of spiritual hype at best, and blatant spiritual deception at worst. Trying to second-guess the return of Christ is dangerous business because it tends toward sensationalism and immobilizes the church in its mission of world evangelism.

Why predict what Christ has already promised? If you trust the promise of His return you won't be tempted to chase such predictions. So, don't get caught up in the sensationalism of the day. Keep your sense and sensibility as you look forward to His return.

THE WORST IS
YET TO COME

The Bible predicts a time of unequaled international distress known as the Great Tribulation. Jesus said, "For then there will be great distress, unequaled from the beginning of the world until now — and never to be equaled again" (Matthew 24:21).

Let the sobering reality of His words sink deep into your heart. The Bible also refers to this time as the time of Jacob's trouble (Jeremiah 30:6, 7), the day of wrath (Isaiah 26:20, 21) and the 70th week of Daniel (Daniel 9:24-27). This period of history will be so horrific in apocalyptic judgments that Jesus said, "Men will faint from terror, apprehensive of what is coming on the world, for the heavenly bodies will be shaken" (Luke 21:26).

Many scholars believe the Great Tribulation will last for seven years, a view based on Daniel's prophecy concerning the 70 weeks (see Daniel 9:24-27). This seven-year period will consist of *two* three and a half year periods.

The first period will be a time of relative peace as the Antichrist builds his empire and enters into a peace treaty with Israel. The latter three-and-a-half-year period will be characterized by the worst unleashing of human suffering that has ever occurred in the history of the world, resulting from the worldwide tyranny of the Antichrist and the judgment of God.

The mysterious 70 weeks of Daniel provides the basis for the seven-year dating of the Great Tribulation. The 70 weeks speak of a literal period of 490 years based on the mathematical equivalent of 70 times 7 years (a prophetic week is 70 years). The 70 weeks concern both comings of the Messiah.

Daniel gives a six-fold purpose for the 70 weeks: "Seventy 'sevens' are decreed for your people and your holy city to finish transgression, to put an end to sin, to atone for wickedness, to bring in everlasting righteousness, to seal up vision and prophecy and to anoint the most holy" (Daniel 9:24). The prophecy unfolds the first and second comings of the Messiah, as well as the rise of the Antichrist:

> *"Know and understand this: From the issuing of the decree to restore and rebuild Jerusalem until the Anointed One, the ruler,*

comes, there will be seven 'sevens,' and sixty-two 'sevens.' It will be rebuilt with streets and a trench, but in times of trouble. After the sixty-two 'sevens,' the Anointed One will be cut off and will have nothing. The people of the ruler who will come will destroy the city and the sanctuary. The end will come like a flood: War will continue until the end, and desolations have been decreed. He will confirm a covenant with many for one 'seven.' In the middle of the 'seven' he will put an end to sacrifice and offering. And on a wing of the temple he will set up an abomination that causes desolation, until the end that is decreed is poured out on him" (Daniel 9:25-27).

J. Dwight Pentecost offers us some helpful insights on this passage. Six promised blessings are related to the two works of the Messiah: His death and His reign. The first three have special reference to the sacrifice of the Messiah, which anticipate removal of sin from the nation. The second three have special reference to the sovereignty of the Messiah, which anticipate the establishment of His reign. The "everlasting righteousness" can only refer to the millennial kingdom promised to Israel.[6]

Historically, we know that 69 of the 70 weeks — 483 years — have already been fulfilled in the time period beginning with the rebuilding of the Jerusalem wall (c. 450 B.C.), after the Jewish remnant returned from the Babylonian exile, and ending with the crucifixion of the Messiah who, in the words of Daniel, would be "cut off" and "have nothing" after the 69 weeks were completed.

The astonishing accuracy of Daniel's prophecy of the exact time of Jesus' death and resurrection is an undeniable testimony to the divine inspiration of Scripture. Only one week, or seven years, is yet to be fulfilled in a literal manner. This will complete God's plan for Israel according to Daniel's 70 weeks.

This final week is the seven-year Great Tribulation. Israel is the focus of God's activity during the Tribulation period resulting in their salvation (see Romans 9-11). That's why the angel tells Daniel that "seventy [weeks] are decreed for your people (Israel) and your holy city (Jerusalem)" (Daniel 9:24).

What will happen during the Great Tribulation? The Bible identifies certain world conditions that will exist during the tribulation period:

1. The rise of globalism will take place under the Antichrist, including the economy, religion and politics, as he seeks to bring the whole world under his control (see 2 Thessalonians 2:1-12; 1 John 2:18; Revelation 13:1-18).

2. Intense persecution will come to those who are courageous enough to accept Christ during the Tribulation. This persecution will consist of economic oppression, the loss of religious freedom, and even imprisonment and death for many (see Matthew 24:9-13; Revelation 6:9-11).

3. A multiplicity of wars, famines and desolations will result from the international conflicts and wars between the Antichrist and the nations that initially oppose him (see Daniel 9:26; Matthew 24:6, 7; Revelation 9:15).

4. A great revival will take place in the nation of Israel, as well as in other nations. The gospel of Christ will continue to be proclaimed during the Tribulation (see Matthew 24:14; Romans 11:25-32; Revelation 14:6, 7).

5. The judgment of God will be unleashed on the Antichrist and his followers. It will reach its climax at the Battle of Armageddon and the second coming of Christ. The judgments are presented in two series of symbols, the seven trumpets (Revelation 8-11) and the seven bowls of wrath (16:1-21).

Perhaps the greatest tragedy that occurs during the Tribulation is the continued disobedience of most of the world. Despite the fact that the eternal gospel will be proclaimed and the judgments of God poured out calling humanity to repentance, the Revelator says:

> The rest of mankind that were not killed by these plagues still did not repent of the work of their hands; they did not stop worshiping demons, and idols of gold, silver, bronze, stone and wood — idols that cannot see or hear or walk. Nor did they repent of their murders, their magic arts, their sexual immorality or their thefts (9:20-21; see also 16:21).

In 1666 a rumor spread throughout England that the world would end that year. The conclusion was drawn from certain biblical students relating the mark of the Beast to that particular year. As the rumor spread, more and more people — commoner and royalty alike — lived under a sense of impending disaster.

That summer, an unusually violent storm arose in western England as Sir Matthew Hale presided as judge in his courtroom. A lawyer present that day wrote the following description of the event:

> All of a sudden the courtroom grew completely dark, though it was still midday. And then the entire courtroom seemed to shake as peals of thunder shook the walls, and bright flashes of lightning momentarily illuminated the room. People inside the courtroom were overcome with fear and, as if by common consent, each fell to his knees and prayed for mercy, believing that the 'terrible day of the Lord' had arrived.[7]

The lawyer noticed, however, that Judge Hale sat unmoved by the events. He continued to take notes of the trial as though nothing out of the ordinary was happening.

The lawyer concluded that Judge Hale's heart was "so stayed on God, that no surprise, however sudden, could discompose him."

When you ponder the prospects of the end of the world, how do you respond? With fear or with faith? Remember that the end of this age means that Jesus Christ will return to rule over all as King of kings and Lord of lords. His coming is given to us as a promise of hope, not as a prediction of doom. The message is,

> "When these things begin to take place, stand up and lift up your heads, because your redemption is drawing near" (Luke 21:28).

TERMINATION OR
TRANSFORMATION?

Human history as we know it will come to an abrupt end at what the Bible calls the Battle of Armageddon (see Ezekiel 38; Joel 3; Zechariah 14; Revelation 14:20; 16:16).

The Hebrew word *harmageddon* can be translated "the hill or mountain of Meggido." It refers to the valley in northern Israel beginning at Meggido and stretching 200 miles south to the Gulf of Aqaba. This valley has been the site of many historic battles. Napoleon referred to it as the most natural battlefield in the world. It is also referred to in the Bible as the Valley of Jehoshaphat, the Valley of Jezreel and the Valley of Decision.

The scenes of Armageddon given by both the Old Testament prophets and the Revelation are horrific in their proportions. The battle is referred to as "the great day of God Almighty" (Revelation 16:14). In one of his visions, the apostle John sees an army of 200 million gathered and sees the blood flowing as high as the horses' bridles. Armageddon, then, represents more than a human war with nations fighting over lands, wealth and resources. It describes the final spiritual conflict between good and evil.

Jesus Christ will return in triumphant glory at Armageddon to destroy the Antichrist and his kingdom, and to establish the eternal kingdom of God. As He promised:

> "For as lightning that comes from the east is visible even in the west, so will be the coming of the Son of Man. Immediately after the distress of those days 'the sun will be darkened, and the moon will not give its light; the stars will fall from the sky, and the heavenly bodies will be shaken.'
>
> "At that time the sign of the Son of Man will appear in the sky, and all the nations of the earth will mourn. They will see the Son of Man coming on the clouds of the sky, with power and great glory. And he will send his angels with a loud trumpet call, and they will gather his elect from the four winds, from one end of the heavens to the other" (Matthew 24:27, 29-31).

After Armageddon, the Antichrist and the False Prophet will be cast into the lake of fire (19:19-21). Paul the apostle tells us that "when the Lord Jesus is revealed from heaven in blazing fire with his powerful angels. . . .

> They will be punished with everlasting destruction and shut out from the presence of the Lord and from the majesty of his power on the day he comes to be glorified in his holy people and to be marveled at among all those who have believed (2 Thessalonians 1:7–10).

Satan will be bound in the Abyss for 1,000 years (Revelation 20:1-10). This thousand-year period is called the Millennium, when Jesus Christ reigns as King over the nations of the world.

Some scholars and ministers debate whether or not the thousand years is literal. Some note the highly symbolic use of numerology in the Revelation and conclude that the number 1,000 probably speaks of the golden age of Christ's glorious reign as opposed to an exact time period.

What a glorious time it will be when the "kingdom of the world has become the kingdom of our Lord and of his Christ, and he will reign for ever and ever" (11:15).

In the final analysis, it doesn't matter whether or not the thousand years speaks of a literal time period — the millennial reign of Jesus Christ is literal and will be an unparalleled time of peace and prosperity for the whole world. Isaiah, the prince of prophets, describes the Millennium this way:

> *"The wolf and the lamb will feed together, and the lion will eat straw like an ox. . . . They will neither harm nor destroy on all my holy mountain"* (65:25).

> *"For the earth will be full of the knowledge of the Lord as the waters cover the sea* (11:9).

> *Many peoples will . . . say, "Come, let us go up to the mountain of the Lord, to the house of the God of Jacob. He will teach us his ways, so that we may walk in his paths."*

> *The law will go out from Zion, the word of the Lord from Jerusalem. He will judge between the nations and will settle disputes for many peoples. They will beat their swords into plowshares and their spears into pruning hooks. Nation will not take up sword against nation, nor will they train for war anymore* (2:3, 4).

The Millennium will conclude with the final judgment of God at what is called the Great White Throne Judgment. The most terrifying scene in the entire Bible is found in Revelation 20:11–15, when John sees a great white throne and before it all who have ever lived, both great and small.

The dead will be judged according to their works—that is, according to their level of spiritual knowledge, to the law of God and to how they responded to the gospel of Christ. The great tragedy is, "If anyone's name was not found written in the book of life, he was thrown into the lake of fire" (v.15).

The concept of eternal separation from God is a troubling proposition to consider. Yet, the Bible tells us that hell is real. More will be said about this later as we move through the Revelation. Let me point out two great truths about the judgment of God:

First, God is merciful. No one will perish unjustly. As Abraham declared when he interceded for Sodom and Gomorrah, "Will not the Judge of all the earth do right?" (Genesis 18:25).

Second, God has made ample provision for every person to be saved and escape the judgment to come. That's why Jesus came to earth the first time. God's gift of salvation is depicted in the Revelation as knowing your name is written in the Lamb's Book of Life.

The promise is given to every believer: "He who overcomes will not be hurt at all by the second death" (Revelation 2:11). The second death is eternal separation from God.

A NEW
WORLD ORDER

After the Millennium, God will re-create the world as we know it. The apostle Peter puts it this way:

But the day of the Lord will come like a thief. The heavens will disappear with a roar; the elements will be destroyed by fire, and the earth and everything in it will be laid bare. . . . That day will bring about the destruction of the heavens by fire, and the elements will melt in the heat. But in keeping with his promise we are looking forward to a new heaven and a new earth, the home of righteousness (2 Peter 3:10, 12b, 13).

This terrestrial ball on which we live is about 25,000 miles in circumference and 8,000 miles in diameter. It is filled with boiling, molten elements. Maybe the unleashing of these elements will cause the earth to become a ball of fire in space as God's purifying process takes place.

Others see in this passage a reference to nuclear war. No one knows for sure how it will happen. But a new earth is our promised inheritance. Regardless of what means God uses, He has promised a new heaven and a new earth.

In his final vision, John catches a glimpse of the new earth. He hears the voice of God thundering from the throne, "I am making everything new!" (Revelation 21:5). The best part of this new eternal home is the full fellowship we will have with God. The Bible says that we will "see His face" (22:4).

No wonder John, after seeing the coming new creation and the New Jerusalem of God, burst forth in anticipation, "Even so, come. Lord Jesus" (22:20, *KJV*). The phrase is in the present tense and means literally, "Be coming, Lord Jesus." In other words, "Carry out Your plan in history in view of Your coming! 'Thy kingdom come, thy will be done' now as well as in the future."

In *World Aflame* Billy Graham comments: "Whatever is not suited for the new life of the new world will be destroyed. This is what some call the end of the world, but the world will never end. It will only be changed into a better world.[8]

A friend once remarked to Mark Twain, "I am worried. The world is coming to an end." "Don't worry about it," replied Twain. "We can get along without it." He was exactly right. We can get along without this old world. God will give us a new world in His time.

HOW THEN
SHOULD WE LIVE

There's no way to consider these prophecies without making a personal response: "Since everything will be destroyed in this way, what kind of people ought you to be? You ought to live holy and godly lives as you look forward to the day of God and speed its coming. . . . So then, dear friends, since you are looking forward to this, make every effort to be found spotless, blameless and at peace with him" (2 Peter 3:11, 14).

Let me point out how not to respond to the message of Christ's return and the end of the age:

1. *Don't get caught up in Rapture fever.* Martin Luther said if he knew Christ would come on Tuesday he would plant an apple tree on Monday. Maintain that sense of mystery about His return.

Don't quit your job or refuse to go to college or fail to prepare yourself for life because you get caught up in the hype and become overly confident that the Rapture is at hand. No one knows the day nor the hour . . . absolutely no one!

2. *Don't follow the sign-seekers.* They love to attach meaning to every intricate detail of the visions of Daniel and the Revelation and to fill the minds of their followers with endless speculations about the future. A Texas evangelist built a case against Ronald Wilson Reagan, claiming he was the Antichrist because each of his three names contained six letters. Quick on his feet, Reagan pointed out that so did the evangelist's name. The evangelist quickly dropped his unfounded and errant theory.

3.   By all means, stay away from the dogmatic debaters. They are the ones who believe their position on Bible prophecy is right and everyone else is wrong. Whatever your beliefs are make sure you remain open to those different from your own. Only then are you really in a position to learn and grow in your faith.

4.   Finally, be on your guard against callous cynicism. This sometimes happens to people who get caught up in the hype of reading the signs of the return of Christ. When things don't unfold like they expect, they become disillusioned and even doubt His promise.

If Jesus doesn't return by Year 2000, you can be sure that some people will be shaken in their faith when the clock strikes 12:01 a.m. on January 1. The apostle Peter hit the problem head-on:

> *First of all, you must understand that in the last days scoffers will come, scoffing and following their own evil desires. They will say, "Where is this 'coming' he promised? Ever since our fathers died, everything goes on as it has since the beginning of creation* (2 Peter 3:3, 4).

When the disciples asked Jesus, "Lord, are you at this time going to restore the kingdom to Israel?" He replied, "It is not for you to know the times or dates the Father has set by His own authority." That's a polite way of saying, "It is none of your concern."

Then He went on to tell them what was important: "But you will receive power . . . and you will be my witnesses . . . to the ends of the earth" (Acts 1:6-8). The point is, don't get caught up in date-setting or sign-seeking. Jesus will return at God's appointed time—not a minute too soon and not a minute too late. How, then, should we live in view of His appearing?

Look up! Jesus said to live with a sense of expectancy for His return, especially when we see the signs of the times being fulfilled on a global scale: "When these things begin to take place, stand up and lift up your heads, because your redemption is drawing near" (Luke 21:28).

✝ When you hear of false christs and false prophets appearing—look up!

✝ When you hear of wars and rumors of wars, and famines, earthquakes and pestilences in many places—look up!

✝ When you read the headlines or watch the evening news and feel depressed—look up!

The Christian should always have an upward gaze instead of a downcast countenance.

Look out! Jesus said, "Open your eyes and look at the fields! They are ripe for harvest" (John 4:35). Leith Anderson estimates that there are 28,000 conversions per day in China (185 million Christians live in China today), 20,000 a day in Africa, 10,000 a day in South America with 50,000 new churches being opened every year.[9]

Missions organizations are putting forth a tremendous effort to evangelize the unreached people groups in the 10/40 Window. The 10/40 Window is home to the majority of the world's unreached peoples.

In October, 1995 an estimated 30 million Christians participated in focused prayer for the evangelization of 100 "Gateway Cities" in the 10/40 Window.

In Kenya, Africa, a gospel team shows Christian films to unreached village people. During a 12-month period the team showed films to 123,000 people. Of those, 42,991 accepted Christ.

According to a report in *Decision* magazine, a billion people heard the gospel during a Global Mission Rally with Billy Graham.[10]

You don't have to do something great for God or be the next international evangelist. You can serve the Lord right where you live, work and play. That's your mission field. Usually, the most effective ministry consists of simple acts of kindness done in the name of Christ.

Martin Luther said, "Every Christian is called to be Christ to his neighbor." That's what Jesus meant when He said, "Whatever you did for one of the least of these brothers of mine, you did for me" (Matthew 25:40).

Look in! Look into your own heart; is Christ there? Has He set up His throne in your heart? The only way to be ready for the future is to be in Christ. The Bible says, "Believe in the Lord Jesus, and you will be saved" (Acts 16:31).

At the end of World War II, England was filled with orphaned children whose parents had died during the war. A social worker was visiting state orphanages to inspect the quality of care being provided. A particular orphanage directed by an elderly couple seemed to have a special grandparent touch of tenderness with each child.

Unlike the other orphanages inspected, this one possessed an unusual climate of peace. The children seemed to be happier and more content than those at other facilities. When the social worker inquired of the couple why this was the case, they said:

Every night we do something special for these children. We tuck each one in bed and put a piece of bread in their hand. They take the bread and clutch it tightly, knowing then that they will not go without something to eat. We kiss each one on the head as we give them the bread and say, "Everything will be okay tomorrow."

In a world of uncertainty God places the Revelation in our hands and says, "Don't worry about the future— everything will be okay tomorrow."

Chapter
3

O world invisible, we view thee,
O world intangible, we touch thee,
O world unknowable, we know thee,
Inapprehensible, we clutch thee!

— Francis Thompson in "The Kingdom of God"

THE THRONE IN HEAVEN

After this I looked, and there before me was a door standing open in heaven. And the voice I had first heard speaking to me like a trumpet said, "Come up here, and I will show you what must take place after this." At once I was in the Spirit, and there before me was a throne in heaven with someone sitting on it (Revelation 4:1, 2).

I'm sure you've heard the saying "He's so heavenly-minded, he's no earthly good." The truth is, the One who was the most heavenly-minded did the most earthly good.

If the Book of Revelation gives us any resource for daily living, it gives us a healthy dose of heavenly-mindedness — what we might call an eternal perspective in a temporal world. This is what the apostle Paul was talking about when he shared how he endured the stress and strains of life:

Therefore we do not lose heart. Though outwardly we are wasting away, yet inwardly we are being renewed day by day. For our light and momentary troubles are achieving for us an eternal glory that far outweighs them all. So we fix our eyes not on what is seen, but on what is unseen. For what is seen is temporary, but what is unseen is eternal (2 Corinthians 4:16-18).

Life without this eternal perspective is lived in a hopeless pessimism expressed in the words of H.G. Wells, "The experiment will be over, the crystals gone, dissolving down the wastepipe."[1] Many people live their lives today in the same kind of pessimism often described in the classical Greco-Roman world:

Death reigned as king of terrors, spoiling men's enjoyment of the present with the intruding thought of the future, so that life could seem a gift not worth receiving, and death in infancy preferable to growing up to the conscious anticipation of having to die.[2]

Such is the case of many of America's youth today. We call them Generation X; but who are they? They are the 38 million young people between the ages of 11 and 30. Psychologically and socially, they are described as being bored with life, disconnected with history and pessimistic about the future.

Advertising Age magazine described Generation X as "that cynical, purple-haired blob watching TV." They confront social phenomena like AIDS, MTV, environmental catastrophes, and the national debt, yet lack the power to cope.[3]

The most important characteristic of Generation X, however, is their deep hunger for God. A rock group sings, "Tell me all your thoughts on God, cause I really want to know."

Secular writer and Generation X spokesman Douglas Coupland articulates the quest for God among Generation X'ers: "My secret is that I need God — that I am sick and can no longer make it alone. I need God to help me give, because I no longer seem capable of giving; to help me be kind, as I no longer seem capable of kindness; to help me love, as I seem beyond being able to love."

Secularism has robbed us of our eternal or spiritual outlook by keeping us so focused on the external world around us. By doing so it ignores the spiritual and the eternal, reducing humanity to little more than the animals.

When we get caught up in secularism we become materialistic, measuring success by the accumulation of wealth and accomplishments of personal goals.

Secularism makes us hedonistic, always seeking for a new thrill through a constant dose of pleasure.

It makes us relativistic in our morals, convinced that there are no absolute values by which to live. Our thinking can become existential causing us to live only in the here and now and lose sight of hope beyond the grave.

What we need today is a new spiritual outlook on life. The philosopher Archimedes said, "Give me a place to stand and I will move the world." That's what the book of Revelation does: it gives us a place to stand in the presence of God so that we can put our lives into perspective.

As a result, we can move our world for the glory of God. Every person looks ahead to the future with a mind-set of either fear or faith. This is what Jesus meant when He said that in the last days "men will faint from terror, apprehensive of what is coming on the world, for the heavenly bodies will be shaken" (Luke 21:26).

But there is a better way. He went on to say, "When these things begin to take place, stand up and lift up your heads, because your redemption is drawing near" (v. 28). The power of an eternal perspective is the ability to look up!

If any people ever needed an eternal perspective it was the early church as the first century drew to a close. They were looking for Christ's return, yet Rome threatened to destroy the church. All of the original 12 apostles had been martyred except John, and he had been exiled to Patmos by the Roman government.

Uncertainty and apprehension filled the air.

In the midst of those uncertain times, the Holy Spirit gave to John the Book of Revelation to reassure His people in times of trouble that God is sovereign. The word *sovereignty* simply means the ultimate rule, power and authority of God over the universe. God controls and directs history to fulfill His purpose.

God is the Almighty. He alone is worthy to be worshiped and obeyed. More importantly, God is sovereign over our personal lives so that we know whatever comes our way, He is watching over us to bring us safely into His eternal kingdom.

In exile John came to see life from heaven's vantage point, and he wants us to have that same perspective so that we can handle anything that comes our way. He learned about the sovereignty of God in a most unusual fashion—he was caught up to heaven in a vision.

This is how he describes his experience: "There before me was a door standing open in heaven. And the voice . . . said, 'Come up here, and I will show you what must take place after this' " (4:1).

John was not the first person in the Bible to catch a glimpse of heaven being opened.

✝ The prophet Ezekiel viewed heaven being opened as he saw visions of God (Ezekiel 1:1).

✝ When Jesus was baptized by John the Baptist in the Jordan River, heaven was opened (Matthew 3:16).

✝ John the Revelator saw heaven open later when Jesus Christ returns in triumphant power at the Battle of Armageddon (19:11).

What does all this about heaven being opened really mean? The fact that heaven is open and not closed tells us that God has prepared a way for us to go to heaven. Jesus said, "I am the door of the sheep" (John 10:7, *KJV*).

The open door of heaven means that God is giving us a glimpse of what life on earth looks like from the balcony of heaven. That's why John was transported into heaven. His vision of the majestic throne of God enables us to view history—past, present and future—from heaven's vantage point. We must look at things from God's perspective.

Believe me, life looks quite different from this angle. As we join the heavenly host around the throne described in John's vision, we too catch a glimpse of one of the most important truths in the entire Bible—the sovereignty of God.

A LOOK AT
THE THRONE

Look at the majesty of the throne that John saw:

And the one who sat there had the appearance of jasper and carnelian. A rainbow, resembling an emerald, encircled the throne. Surrounding the throne were twenty-four other thrones, and seated on them were twenty-four elders. They were dressed in white and had crowns of gold on their heads. From the throne came flashes of lightning, rumblings and peals of thunder. Before the throne, seven lamps were blazing. These are the seven spirits of God. Also before the throne there was what looked like a sea of glass, clear as crystal.

In the center, around the throne, were four living creatures, and they were covered with eyes, in front and in back. The first living creature was like a lion, the second was like an ox, the third had a face like a man, the fourth was like a flying eagle (Revelation 4:3-7).

If you're like me you probably feel somewhat overwhelmed by the majesty of his vision and by the incredibly strange characters in the scene. But it's not as complicated as it might look at first glance. Let me explain the imagery.

Start with the throne itself. The throne of God is the chief symbol of the Revelation and is referred to 45 times in this book, compared to only 15 times in the rest of the New Testament. It is referenced in every chapter except 2, 8 and 9. This tells us that the throne is very important to our lives.

The royal throne depicts God's sovereign rule over the universe. The psalmist proclaimed, "God reigns over the nations; God is seated on his holy throne" (Psalm 47:8).

All of history must be viewed from the aspect of the throne. Washington is not in control, Beijing is not in control, Jerusalem is not in control, Moscow is not in control. God, and God alone, ultimately controls the outcome of history.

The fact that He reigns supreme gives us comfort, strength and faith in every circumstance. If God can take care of this vast universe, God can take care of you and me.

That's the lesson God wants you to learn from this incredible vision: He will take care of you!

Not only does John see the majestic throne of God, he also sees God himself seated on the throne. It is one thing to see the throne, but quite another to see God himself. The throne assures us that nothing happens or exists apart from God's will. As John gropes for words to describe to us the majestic glory of God, notice that he never gets overly familiar with God. He never tries to describe the form of the Lord. God remains shrouded in the mystery of His majesty, lest we loose our sense of the awe of God.

John's vision of God is awe-inspiring. God's glory resembles that of a jasper stone, clear and dazzling like a diamond; and the carnelian stone, red in its color, calling to mind the blood covenant of Christ's sacrifice for the sins of the world. A beautiful deep-green emerald rainbow shines around the throne. God gave the rainbow to Noah as a sign of His covenant-faithfulness.

From the throne comes lightning and thunder. These phenomena are mentioned four times in Revelation. They describe the judgment of God and His promise to deliver His people. Thunder and lightning shook the heavens at Mount Sinai when Moses received the Law and saw the infinite glory of God (Exodus 19:16).

The point is clear: Just as God delivered Israel from Egyptian bondage and the dangers of the wilderness, God will deliver His people today from all harm and threat of the antichrist system. John's vision continues . . . and represents the full, complete ministry of the Holy Spirit. In front of the throne appears a sea of glass. What a marvelous picture. In the midst of everything that John sees, the sea of glass means that all is calm and peaceful. When you come to see and to believe in the sovereignty of God in your life, your emotions will be like this sea of glass — tranquil and calm in a world of uncertainty.

Around the throne John stood in the presence of some fascinating creatures. Let's meet them. First, he sees 24 other thrones occupied by 24 elders. Who are they? They are the people of God. Historically, the number 12 represents the people of God.

For example, in the Revelation we read about the 12 tribes of Israel, the 12 apostles, the 12 gates of the New Jerusalem, 12 angels at the gates, and 12 foundations of the city.

The length and width of the city is 12,000 stadia and 144,000 people are sealed by God in the Revelation.

The number 24 is a multiple of 12 and symbolizes the complete covenant community — Old Testament believers represented by the 12 tribes of Israel; and believers who have lived since the time of Christ, represented by the 12 apostles.

Let me give a little more background on this numerology. King David appointed 24 divisions of the priests (1 Chronicles 24) and 24 divisions of the Levite singers (1 Chronicles 25) in preparation for the building of the new Temple.

Biblical elders are those who exercise spiritual leadership and whose responsibility it is to serve the church (see Acts 15:6; 20:28).

The elders John saw in heaven were awarded crowns of gold, which they gladly cast before the throne in honor to God, and white robes, which signifies that they are righteous in Christ. It is easy, then, to see that this figure of the 24 elders represents everyone who has faith in God and confesses Jesus Christ as Lord.

THE
VICTORIOUS CHURCH

Think with me about the imagery of the white robes. They represent the righteousness of God's people (see Revelation 19:8). If you're like me you don't feel too righteous at times. But righteousness is not a work, it's a gift.

The great truth of the Christian faith is that God gives us the righteousness of Jesus as a gift of grace when we believe in Him. We call this justification. Paul said:

> That I may gain Christ and be found in him, not having a righteousness of my own that comes from the law, but that which is through faith in Christ — the wonderful gift of righteousness that comes from God and is by faith (Philippians 3:8b, 9).

Calvary is the place of the "great exchange." At Calvary, when Jesus died for our sins, "God made him who had no sin to be sin for us, so that in him we might become the righteousness of God" (2 Corinthians 5:21).

This means that when you accept by faith Jesus' death as the payment of your sins, God takes away your sins and gives you the righteousness of Jesus. That's why I call it the great exchange — our sins are removed and replaced with His righteousness! Not only are we dressed in white, we are given glorious crowns to wear.

Let me point out an important feature we should know about these crowns of gold. The Greek word used for crown here is *stephanos.* In ancient times the *stephanos* was given as the victor's crown in athletic competition, or as a token of honor for distinguished public service. It is not the word used to describe the crown a king or queen wears. That kind of crown is called a *diadem*. That's the kind of crown Jesus wears as the King of kings. The *stephanos* was a garland of fresh flowers, sometimes laden with gold, given as an award of victory or honor.

Christ will reward his people for their steadfast faithfulness. Look at this idea of the *stephanos* in the New Testament. Christ has promised us a crown that is incorruptible (1 Corinthians 9:25), a crown of righteousness (2 Timothy 4:8), a crown of life (James 1:12), and a crown of glory (1 Peter 5:4).

Success in life is not measured by prosperity, power, position or pleasure. True success will be to stand before the Christ of all eternity as He places the victor's crown around your neck, saying, "Well done, good and faithful servant. Enter into the joy of the Lord, the kingdom prepared for you since the foundation of the world!"(see Matthew 25:21, 23, 34).

In December, 1996 international industrialists David Suna and John Tu sold 80 percent of the world's largest manufacturer of computer memory products, Kingston Technology Corporation, for $1.5 billion. These two men decided to share their windfall with their employees. The average bonus payment their workers received was a little more than $75,000. Suna summarized their decision: "To share our success with everybody is the most joy we can have."

Well, that's what Jesus is going to do for us in eternity. He's going to share the rewards of His grace with us. If that isn't enough to make your cup run over, John goes on to describe four mighty angels that he calls "living creatures" around that throne. Who are they? They are the cherubim of Ezekiel's vision (Ezekiel 1).

They first appeared in Eden when Adam and Eve left the garden. With flaming swords they are seen guarding the way to the tree of life: "After he drove the man out, he placed on the east side of the Garden of Eden cherubim and a flaming sword flashing back and forth to guard the way to the tree of life" (Genesis 3:24).

Later, we see them hovering over the ark of the covenant, fashioned out of pure gold and embroidered in the veil in Solomon's temple. They stand as a barrier between us and God. They remind us that God is holy and we are sinful. As long as the cherubim stand guard, God is unapproachable.

But there's more to these creatures. Their appearance is captivating. Their faces represent all creation before the throne. The lion with his glory, the ox with his strength, the man with his intelligence and spirituality, and the eagle in his grandeur are all the most superior in their categories.

Each cherub is covered with wings and they are swift to carry out God's will. They are also covered with eyes, and they see all that takes place in heaven and on earth. These cherubim also depict the ministry of Jesus Christ. The early church leader Irenaeus was the first person to make this observation.

✝ He said the lion shows Christ as the royal Son of God who fulfills God's covenant with David.

✝ The ox depicts Jesus as the burden-bearer, who laid down His life for us.

✝ The man represents Christ in His incarnation, for "the Word became flesh and made his dwelling among us" (John 1:14).

✝ And the eagle represents Jesus sending the Holy Spirit to hover over the church.

Another observation needs to be made. When the Israelites wandered in the wilderness, they camped around the Tabernacle in groups of three tribes on each of the four sides. The four banners displayed over these encampments bore the images of these same four faces.

All of this tells us that around the throne of God all creation is represented. It says that we have access to God because of the ministry of Jesus Christ, our Great High Priest, who ever lives to make intercession for us.

Cherubim lead all of heaven in worship. They sing two great songs. First, they celebrate the sovereignty of God. "Day and night they never stop saying: 'Holy, holy, holy is the Lord God Almighty, who was, and is, and is to come'" (Revelation 4:8).

Then they proclaim that God is creator: "You are worthy, our Lord and God, to receive glory and honor and power, for you created all things, and by your will they were created and have their being" (v. 11).

Let me encourage you to take the time in life to allow the cherubim to lead you into worship. Do not neglect to give God praise for His assurance that He is sovereign in your life and that He is your Creator, your Redeemer and your Father. The purpose of the Revelation is to lead us to the place where we can see the greatness of God and proclaim His praise.

When Handel composed the *Messiah* after 24 days of seclusion, someone asked him how he was able to write such a brilliant masterpiece. He replied, "I saw heaven open before me, and God Almighty seated on His holy throne."

As majestic as John's vision has been up to this point, there is more. Now he notices a seven-sealed scroll in the hand of God. What is this mysterious scroll, and what does it tell about the future?

THE SEVEN-SEALED
SCROLL

A sealed scroll was used in two ways in the ancient world. First, a sealed scroll was a document containing sensitive material and could be opened only by the owner. A Roman last will and testament was sealed with six seals.

In John's vision the seven-sealed scroll represents God's ultimate plan for humanity to bring all things together under Christ. (Remember that the number seven means completion.)

The fact that the scroll is sealed tells us that the contents are mysterious and hidden, as in the case of Daniel who was instructed to *seal* his prophecies "until the time of the end" (Daniel 12:4). The sealed contents also indicate that God still has much to accomplish in history.

As the seals are opened, God's plan for us is seen in a series of judgments and blessings: seven seals, trumpets and bowls. Notice great similarities in these three series of judgments.

The horrific events announced seem to build with intensity with the opening of each seal. They are followed by the trumpet judgments. Finally the judgments come to a climax with the seven last plagues.

The point is that the history of the church age, beginning with Pentecost and ending with the return of Christ, will be a time of upheaval. Jesus said,

> *"You will hear of wars and rumors of wars, but see to it that you are not alarmed. Such things must happen, but the end is still to come. Nation will rise against nation, and kingdom against kingdom. There will be famines and earthquakes in various places. All these are the beginning of birth pain"* (Matthew 24:6-8).

He also told about persecution to come, the falling away of some from Christ and the increase of wickedness in the last days. But in the midst of chaotic world conditions we are called to be faithful to Christ and to minister His gospel to others.

He said, "He who stands firm to the end will be saved. And this gospel of the kingdom will be preached in the whole world as a testimony to all nations, and then the end will come" (Matthew 24:13, 14). That is good news! We must be faithful and we must minister to others.

The main thrust of the seven seals, the seven trumpets and the seven bowls of wrath is to remind us that God is directing history toward His ultimate plan. Remember that the number seven signifies completion. That's why the seventh trumpet and the seventh bowl announce the finished work of God.

This is how John describes it: "The seventh angel sounded his trumpet, and there were loud voices in heaven, which said: 'The kingdom of the world has become the kingdom of our Lord and of his Christ, and he will reign for ever and ever' " (Revelation 11:15).

After that, "the seventh angel poured out his bowl into the air, and out of the temple came a loud voice from the throne, saying, 'It is done!' " (16:17).

Does that remind you of anything? It is the same message Jesus shouted from the cross when He was crucified: "It is finished!"

These very words were the victor's cry given by a Roman general when he saw that his troops were on the verge of winning a military battle. As the victory was sure, overlooking the battlefield he would shout, "It is finished!" Every soldier knew that victory was at hand.

This is the message of Revelation: Victory is at hand. What a message of assurance—peace and victory! As history rolls on God is really in control and He will complete His plan for the world. What is God doing in the world? The Bible tells us clearly what God has planned:

> *And he made known to us the mystery of his will according to his good pleasure, which he purposed in Christ, to be put into effect when the times will have reached their fulfillment — to bring all things in heaven and on earth together under one head, even Christ* (Ephesians 1:9, 10).

When Jesus Christ returns and His kingdom is established, we will finally understand the meaning of His words, "It is finished!" Only Jesus Christ, the Lord of humanity, can bring us into God's wonderful plan.

Suddenly, in dramatic fashion, He steps on the scene in John's vision, takes the scroll from the hand of God and breaks the seals. As the seals are broken history marches on toward eternity with God. John tells us what he saw:

> *I wept and wept because no one was found who was worthy to open the scroll or look inside. Then one of the elders said to me, "Do not weep! See, the Lion of the tribe of Judah, the Root of David, has triumphed. He is able to open the scroll and its seven seals."*

> *Then I saw a Lamb, looking as if it had been slain, standing in the center of the throne, encircled by the four living creatures and the elders. He had seven horns and seven eyes, which are the seven spirits of God sent out into all the earth. He came and took the scroll from the right hand of him who sat on the throne* (Revelation 5:4-7).

Now, Jesus steps forth as the central figure of the drama and His appearance is captivating.

THE LION WHO IS
A LAMB

What a paradox—the lion who is a lamb. The angel announces the entrance of the lion of the tribe of Judah and a lamb steps onto the stage. The Lion of the tribe of Judah is a messianic title referring to the Davidic covenant and picturing Jesus in his conquest over death, hell and the grave. The imagery of the Lamb draws our attention back to the Passover Lamb in Egypt.

In these two pictures Isaiah's conquering King and his suffering Servant come together in Jesus (see Isaiah 42:1-5; 53:4-6). The Lamb is mentioned 30 times in Revelation. The people of God sing a new song celebrating His atonement on the cross, saying, "You are worthy . . . for you redeemed us *by your blood*" (see 5:9).

Whatever picture you may have in your mind of Jesus, always see Him as the Lamb of God who takes away the sins of the world.

Notice that in John's vision no one is able, or qualified, to open the seven-sealed scroll. Only Jesus is worthy. He alone has all authority as King of kings to shape and control the destiny of the world. At Armageddon, Jesus is portrayed as the Lamb who triumphs in the great and final conflict between good and evil.

What do we need to know about Jesus as the Lamb?

First, we see the Lamb slain. Literally "with its throat cut." He has been sacrificed, yet He is alive. That's what He told John in the first vision of the book, "I was dead, and behold I am alive for ever and ever!"(1:18).

Next we see the Lamb standing. He is in the center of the

throne, which tells us that He is equal with God the Father. The fact that He is standing speaks of his unfinished work of judgment.

In other places the Bible places Him as our high priest seated at the right hand of God. He is seated because the work of salvation was finished at the cross. But here we see Him standing as He judges the world and reaps the harvest of the last days.

This Lamb is strong. This is depicted in seven horns. A horn is used repeatedly in the Bible as a symbol of power and authority. Since He has seven horns we know He has all authority and absolute power.

Finally, the Lamb is searching. John describes Him as having seven eyes, which represent His all-knowing power. When I read this I can't help but ask, *What is the Lamb searching for?* He is searching the world for those who are lost. Jesus works through believers today "to seek and to save those who are lost" (see Luke 19:10).

Some people describe their Christian experience by saying, "I found the Lord." The Lord has never been lost! The Lord found *us!* He left heaven and came for us. Religion is man's effort to find God. Christianity is the story of God looking for humanity in the person of Jesus Christ.

The many eyes on the Lamb remind us of the fact that God knows who we are and where we are in life. God sees us. A line in a popular song says, "God is watching us from a distance." But the truth is, "His eye is on the sparrow, and I know He watches over me."

God isn't watching from a distance, far removed from life; He is watching intently to care for your every need. The Lamb is also searching for something in our lives. The Lamb is searching for a faithful church. That's why Jesus asked the question, "When the Son of Man comes, will he find faith on the earth?" (Luke 18:8).

The Lord doesn't look for perfection, but He does look for faithfulness in us. We can't be perfect, but we can be faithful. The Revelation is a call to faithfulness to Christ, and to the body and cause of Christ in the world. "This calls for patient endurance and faithfulness on the part of the saints" (13:10). The most beautiful portrait of Jesus you'll ever have is a mental image of the Lamb of God.

The largest crowd Spurgeon ever addressed came the night he spoke in the Crystal Palace to 23,654 people. A mutiny had occurred in India protesting Britain's rule over that land, and a service of national humiliation was planned. Spurgeon was selected to deliver the sermon.

The night before the service, he went to the Crystal Palace to test the acoustics, since the building was not constructed with religious services in mind. As he stood on the platform he repeated the verse, "Behold the Lamb of God, which takes away the sin of the world."

His words were heard by a man working somewhere in the building. The man came to Spurgeon several days later to say that the verse had touched his heart, and he had come to know the Lord Jesus Christ.[4]

So John watches the Lamb take the scroll from God's hand in dramatic fashion. He alone has the right to open the scroll since He is the Son of God. As the Lamb prepares to open the scroll, all of heaven bursts forth with praise in a series of three majestic songs.

First, the redeemed sing a new song of praise. In the Old Testament a new song celebrated a new act of divine deliverance or blessing. The deliverance from sin through

Christ's sacrificial death is the theme of our song (Revelation 5:9–14).

> *And they sang a new song: "You are worthy to take the scroll and to open its seals, because you were slain, and with your blood you purchased men for God from every tribe and language and people and nation. You have made them to be a kingdom and priests to serve our God, and they will reign on the earth."*

Then the angels of God join in:

> *Then I looked and heard the voice of many angels, numbering thousands upon thousands, and ten thousand times ten thousand. They encircled the throne and the living creatures and the elders. In a loud voice they sang: "Worthy is the Lamb, who was slain, to receive power and wealth and wisdom and strength and honor and glory and praise!"*

Finally, all creation joins the mighty chorus:

> *Then I heard every creature in heaven and on earth and under the earth and on the sea, and all that is in them, singing: "To him who sits on the throne and to the Lamb be praise and honor and glory and power, for ever and ever!" The four living creatures said, "Amen," and the elders fell down and worshiped.*

When we worship God, we join this universal cosmic symphony. The psalmist reminds us that "all the families of the nations will bow down before him" (Psalm 22:27). Again he says, "Let the rivers clap their hands, let the mountains sing together for joy" (98:8).

The prophet declared that "the mountains and hills will burst into song before you, and all the trees of the field will clap their hands" (Isaiah 55:12). Jesus said, "The rocks will cry out"(see Luke 19:40).

The purpose of all creation is to bring glory to God. Now here's the application to our lives: When we find ourselves fearful, uncertain and uptight about our circumstances we need to take a visit through that open door into heaven. We need to behold the throne of God and see His glory.

The great God of eternity is our heavenly Father who loves us with an everlasting love. He holds us in the palm of His hand and He assures us that He is in control of everything that happens in our lives. When we look at life from the vantage point of heaven, we too can be filled with joyful songs of praise because God is in control. Our hearts rejoice as we sing and leap for joy!

Remember the sea of glass we saw before the throne? That symbol describes the condition of our heart and emotions when we really believe that God is in control. The sea of glass is a portrait of the perfect peace God gives us when we trust Him to take care of every situation we face in life.

All of this symbolism is inspiring, but how do we make the connection between this vision and ordinary, everyday life?

GETTING
CONNECTED

As we ponder the awesome scene of the throne of God, the seven-sealed scroll and the Lamb, we learn first and foremost that the *God who is sovereign over prophetic history is also sovereign over your personal life.* The sovereignty of God is a fantastic promise for your own life. He is in control.

"And we know that in all things God works for the good of those who love him, who have been called according to his purpose. For those God foreknew he also predestined to be conformed to the likeness of his Son" (Romans 8:28, 29).

This means that God is in charge of your life. You don't work for God; God is working in you! As Paul said, "Being confident of this, that he who began a good work in you will carry it on to completion until the day of Christ Jesus" (Philippians 1:6).

Now, the concept of sovereignty doesn't mean that God causes everything that happens in your life. Far from it. But it does mean that God works all things that happen to you and around you together for your good. He does it the same way that a master craftsman uses the multi-colored yarns to weave a beautiful tapestry.

Corrie ten Boom tried to put her own sufferings into perspective after having survived Hitler's death camp. Her anguish and hardships were unbelievable, yet she came through it with a victorious spirit. In her autobiography *Tramp for the Lord,* Corrie shares this anonymous poem:

My life is but a weaving, between my God and me.
I do not choose the colors, He worketh steadily.
Oftimes He weaveth sorrow, and I in foolish pride,
Forget He sees the upper, and I the underside.
Not till the loom is silent, and shuttles cease to fly,
Will God unroll the canvas and explain the reason why.
The dark threads are as needful in the skillful Weaver's hand,
As the threads of gold and silver in the pattern He has planned.[5]

That's the sovereignty of God at work in our lives. So the next time you can't make much sense out of your life, remember this one powerful truth about God: "[He] works out everything in conformity with the purpose of his will" (Ephesians 1:11).

The same God who sits on this magnificent, eternal throne, who rules over all creation, and who directs the course of nature and history also reigns supreme in your life. This means that you can trust Him with everything in your life, for He will never disappoint you.

There's something else we learn as we stand before the throne: *Jesus Christ is both the Savior of the world and Lord of humanity.* In John's vision the Lamb stands triumphantly at the center of the throne.

When the 24 elders fell down in worship and laid their crowns before the throne, they declared, "Our Lord and God." Every Roman citizen had to declare, "Caesar is Lord," as they pledged their loyalty and hailed Emperor Domitian as divine. But the early Christians refused to make this confession. While Rome confessed "Caesar is Lord," the church proclaimed, "Jesus is Lord."

For that creed they lived and for that creed they died. When we lose the sense of the lordship of Christ in our lives we fall into the trap of what Dietrich Bonhoeffer called "cheap grace."[6] He warns us that cheap grace is the deadly enemy of the church.

Cheap grace is grace sold in the marketplace like discounted goods. Cheap grace is grace as a doctrine, a principle, a system. Cheap grace is intellectual assent without true faith.

Cheap grace means the justification of sin without the justification of the sinner. Cheap grace is the preaching of forgiveness without requiring repentance, baptism without church discipline, communion without confession, absolution without personal confession.

Cheap grace is grace without discipleship, grace without a cross, grace without Jesus Christ, living and incarnate. What we need is the costly grace of discipleship. Costly grace is the hidden treasure in a field for which a man sells all to possess. Costly grace is the pearl of great price a merchant will sell all to purchase. Costly grace is the kingly rule of Christ that causes a person to be willing to lose all things in order to gain Christ. Costly grace is the incarnation of God.

✝ It's costly because it calls us to follow, but it's grace because we follow Jesus Christ.

✝ It's costly because it costs us our lives, but it's grace because it gives us abundant life.

✝ It's costly because it condemns sin, but it's grace because it justifies the sinner.

✝ It's costly because it demands submission to the yoke of Christ, but it's grace because He said, "My yoke is easy and my burden is light" (Matthew 11:30).

✝ It's costly because it cost God His only Son, but it's grace because He did not consider Him too high a price to pay for us.

There is a throne in heaven where God rules supreme. As we think about that throne, we gain *an eternal perspective which brings a sense of peace even in troubled times.*

We can rejoice whatever the circumstances. We can respond to the hardships of life as either victims or victors. Victims become bitter, cynical and defeated. Victors, however, release their faith enabling them to become larger than life.

Haralan Papov spent 13 years in a Communist prison because of his faith in Christ. During one stint of solitary confinement he wrote:

> I was alone for 10 days. I felt so close to God in solitary confinement that I spent the time in praise and worship.

Such close communion with God; I talked with Him. He comforted me. It was a spiritual feast for me. During this time, I received new strength, though my body was wasted away to nothing. Tears of joy ran down my face. Here in the DS prison, alone and with nothing, I had everything — Christ. Stripped of everything, without any worldly distractions, I found a deep and beautiful communion with God. Joy and peace flooded my soul. My body ached with starvation but my spirit has never been closer to God. Lying starved, alone and too weak to move; I felt I could reach out to God and be taken in His arms.[7]

Have you surrendered your life to Christ's lordship? When you do, you will find a joy unspeakable and full of glory.

What about the throne in your heart? Is the Lamb at the center of your life? Have you taken your place with the 24 elders as a follower of Jesus?

You too must bow before Him, cast your crowns of accomplishments at His feet and declare, "Lord, You are worthy!"

Chapter

4

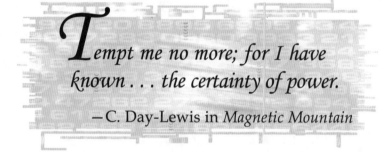

Tempt me no more; for I have known . . . the certainty of power.

—C. Day-Lewis in *Magnetic Mountain*

THEY OVERCAME

*They overcame him by the blood of the Lamb
and by the word of their testimony; they did
not love their lives so much as to shrink from
death* (Revelation 12:11).

The Irish orator, writer and statesman, Edmund Burke (1729-1797) said, "Our antagonist is our helper. He that wrestles with us strengthens our muscles and sharpens our skills."

Apocalypse! Prophecy! Things to come! We have antagonists in the spiritual realm. We struggle with the conflicting forces of fear and faith, of love and hate, of obedience and disobedience, of good and evil. The conflict is around us and within us.

Our greatest and primary struggle is an inward struggle. We can identify with Paul the apostle: "I do not understand what I do. For what I want to do I do not do, but what I hate I do. For I have the desire to do what is good, but I cannot carry it out" (Romans 7:15, 18).

Sir Edwin Arnold, author of *The Light of Asia,* told the students at Harvard College: "In 1776 you conquered your fathers. In 1861 you conquered your brothers. Now the next great victory is to conquer yourselves."

That's the struggle we all face. Mark Twain said, "I've had more trouble with myself than any man I've ever met." The inward battle involves a battle with our flesh.

What is the flesh, anyway? The Greek word Paul uses is *sarx,* which refers to the sin nature. Freud called it, in psychological terms, the *id.* This part of us seeks to avoid pain, relieve tension, and obtain pleasure.

The sin nature is a powerful force within us all. It is inherited from Adam (Romans 5:12), is bent on self-fulfillment (1 John 2:16), is rebellious toward the law of God (Romans 8:6-8), and drives us toward immoral living (Galatians 5:19-21). The sin nature within us all is tempted to follow the world system. John says:

> Do not love the world or anything in the world. If anyone loves the world, the love of the Father is not in him. For everything in the world – the cravings of sinful man, the lust of his eyes and the boasting of what he has and does – comes not from the Father but from the world (1 John 2:15, 16).

Be honest about it – we all have to deal with the pull of the world. We feel the force of the attitudes, values, beliefs, philosophy of life, and lifestyle of the world. The question is, Can we win the war against the sin nature?

Yes! We can overcome the allurements of the world and weakness of the sin nature by the power of Christ who lives in our hearts. "The one who is in you, is greater than the one who is in the world" the Bible says (1 John 4:4, *KJV*).

"This is the victory that has overcome the world, even our faith" (5:4).

Do you ever wonder why this spiritual conflict exists? The Bible tells us in no uncertain terms that we have an adversary. The Book of Revelation identifies this adversary as "that ancient serpent called the devil, or Satan, who leads the whole world astray" (12:9).

Are you kidding me? you may be asking. *Do you really expect me to believe in the devil?* Well, the Bible tells us over and over that the devil not only exists, he is our enemy. There is more to this spiritual conflict than meets the eye.

Paul describes it: "For our struggle is not against flesh and blood, but against the rulers, against the authorities, against the powers of this dark world and against the spiritual forces of evil in the heavenly realms" (Ephesians 6:12). We all know about the inward struggle with the sin nature. But I'm not sure we are as aware of the outward struggle we face in the spiritual realm.

A LOOK AT

THE DARK SIDE

Victor Hugo said, "A good general must penetrate the brain of his enemy." Field Marshall Montgomery, World War II commander of the allied forces in the North African campaign, often quoted this Chinese proverb: "If you know yourself and your adversary clearly, then in a hundred battles you will win a hundred times."

That's exactly what Paul meant when he wrote "in order that Satan might not outwit us. For we are not unaware of his schemes" (2 Corinthians 2:11). The word *schemes* means strategies, tactics, plans, purposes, cunning. It is important at this point to review what the Bible teaches about Satan and his method of operation. Satan's diabolical nature is reflected in the names given to him in Scripture.

He is called *Apollyon*, the destroyer (Revelation 9:11) and *Beelzebub*, the worthless one (Matthew 9:34; 10:25; 12:24).

He is the *deceiver*, which is the first and last Biblical portraits given of him (Revelation 12:9; 20:8–10).

He is the *Dragon*, because of his fierceness (Revelation 12:7), and the *Evil One*, or *Wicked One* (Matthew 13:19, 38; 1 John 2:13.14).

The devil is the *Father of Lies* (John 8:44), the *god of this age* (2 Corinthians 4:4), a *murderer from the beginning* (John 8:44), the *prince of demons,* and the *prince of the power of this world* (Matthew 9:34; Luke 22:53; John 16:11; Ephesians 2:2).

Satan, which means "adversary" or "opposing spirit," is used 18 times in the Old Testament and 35 times in the New Testament. This aspect of his character is shown in Zechariah 3:1; Luke 10:18; 22:31.

The title *devil* speaks of him as being frightful in appearance, wicked in action, horrible in manner, and monstrous in effect. He is the *ancient serpent* (Genesis 3:1; Revelation 12); and the *tempter* (Matthew 4:1-11; 1 Thessalonians 3:5).

Most frequently, he is simply called the *devil,* which means "accuser, slanderer, or deceiver" (see Revelation 12:10; Matthew 13:39). The Greek root word *diabolos* means "a false witness."

Satan's work is carried out in the world through what the Bible calls demons. Demons are fallen angels who have pledged their allegiance to Satan, the prince of demons, in opposition to God. Their sinister activity is focused on destroying all humanity, the object of God's redeeming love.

Old Testament people were forbidden to worship "great idols" or "demons" (see Leviticus 17:7); yet we find them sacrificing "their sons and their daughters to demons" (Psalm 106:37; Deuteronomy 32:17).

The New Testament provides a thorough profile of evil with 80 references to demons, six to evil spirits, and 23 to unclean spirits.

We need to avoid two equally harmful errors concerning the dark side: overstating the devil's work, which causes spiritual hysteria, and underestimating his existence and work. Satanic assaults against the church are real.

As our enemy, he perverts the Scripture, opposes God's work, hinders the gospel, accuses the brethren, tempts to sin, works lying wonders, appears as an angel of light, brings false teaching into the church, and sows discord among the people of God. The greatest tragedy of all is that he "leads the whole world astray" (Revelation 12:9).

Perhaps you are saying, "Wait a minute. I'm not really sure about all this talk about spiritual warfare. To answer the question, let me share this excellent piece that someone sent me. I wish I knew the author.

If I Were the Devil

If I were the Prince of Darkness I'd want to engulf the whole world in darkness, and I'd have a third of its real estate and four-fifths of its population. But I wouldn't be happy until I had seized the ripest apple on the tree — thee.

So I'd set about however necessary to take over the United States. I'd subvert the churches first. I'd begin with a campaign of whispers. With the wisdom of a serpent I would whisper to you as I whispered to Eve, "Do as you please!" To the young I would whisper that the Bible is a myth. I would convince them that man created God instead of the other way around. I would confide that what's bad is good and what's good is square. And the old I would teach people to pray after me, "Our father, which art in Washington."

And then I'd get organized. I'd educate authors in how to make lurid literature exciting so that anything else would be dull and uninteresting. I'd put dirtier movies on TV. I'd peddle narcotics to whom I could. I'd sell alcohol to ladies and gentlemen of distinction. I'd tranquilize the rest with pills.

If I were the devil I'd depict families at war with themselves, churches at war with themselves, and nations at war with themselves until each in its turn was consumed. And with promises of higher ratings I'd have the mesmerizing media fanning the flames.

If I were the devil I'd encourage schools to refine young intellects but neglect to discipline emotions — just let those run wild until before you knew it you'd have to have drug-sniffing dogs and metal detectors at every schoolhouse door.

Within a decade I'd have prisons overflowing. I'd have judges promoting pornography. Soon I could evict God from the courthouse, from the schoolhouse, and then from the houses of congress.

And in the churches I would substitute psychology for religion and make it a science. I would lure priests and pastors into misusing boys and girls and church money.

If I were the devil I'd make the symbol of Easter an egg and the symbol of Christmas a bottle. If I were the devil I'd take from those who have and give to those who wanted until I had killed the incentive of the ambitious.

And what will you bet, I could get entire states to promote gambling as the way to get rich. I would caution against extremes in hard work, in patriotism, in moral conduct. I would convince the young that marriage is old-fashioned; that swinging is more fun; that what you see on TV is the way to be. And thus I could undress you in public and I could lure you into bed with diseases for which there is no cure.

If I were the devil I'd keep on doing what he's now doing.

The point is this: Spiritual warfare is real and it touches every aspect of life on earth. Here is where the Book of Revelation comes in. It gives us much-needed insight into this spiritual war. Let me show you something important about how the Revelation is written from a literary standpoint. It is divided into two primary sections:

✝ **Section One (1:1 – 11:19)** presents the conflict of the church in the world from an earthly or historical view, focusing on God's protection of the church and Israel.

✝ **Section Two (12:1 – 22:21)** presents the underlying conflict between the church and the world system through the subtle work of the Dragon (Satan). Since Satan cannot directly war with Christ, he attacks the church through four primary means:

(1) the beast out of the sea, who is the Antichrist to come and the spirit of antichrist already at work in the world today;

(2) the beast out of the earth, the False Prophet who is to come, and the spirit of false religion that we can see in the world today;

(3) Mystery Babylon the Great, which represents religious and political persecution of the people of God;

(4) the mark of the Beast, which represents the terrors of economic persecution today, and the global economy used by the Antichrist during the Great Tribulation.

These form the four enemies of the church found throughout the Revelation. They are present today and have been since the church was born on the Day of Pentecost. The impact of these enemies will be fulfilled in global proportions during the Great Tribulation period.

Now for the good news: *Jesus Christ will destroy the Dragon and his hordes when He comes in power at Armageddon. The triumphant Lord and His church will rule and reign together for all eternity.*

This is why John uses the word *overcomer* to describe believers in the Revelation. To overcome means to conquer, to win in a conflict, to prevail over an enemy. The Book of Revelation spells victory on every side. In it we see the victory of God as He completes His sovereign will for the world, the victory of Christ in His eternal reign, and the victory of the church against her enemies.

Revelation contains eight wonderful promises to the overcomers: in 2:7, 11, 17, 26; 3:5, 12, 21; and 21:7. I hope you will take the time to look up these references and see what God has promised you as an overcomer.

A MARVELOUS
SIGN IN HEAVEN

Take a closer look at this spiritual war and see how you can be more than a conqueror. The following passage is one of the most fascinating visions in the Revelation. Notice that this theme of spiritual warfare is set in a larger context.

Chapters 12-14 provide an overview of the entire church age, beginning with Christ's incarnation (12:1-5) and ending with His second coming (14:14-20). Chapter 12 gives us particular insight into the spiritual war the devil is waging against the people of God. This is what John said he saw:

> A great and wondrous sign appeared in heaven: a woman clothed with the sun, with the moon under her feet and a crown of twelve stars on her head. She was pregnant and cried out in pain as she was about to give birth. Then another sign appeared in heaven: an enormous red dragon with seven heads and ten horns and seven crowns on his heads. His tail swept a third of the stars out of the sky and flung them to the earth. The dragon stood in front of the woman who was about to give birth, so that he might devour her child the moment it was born. She gave birth to a son, a male child, who will rule all the nations with an iron scepter. And her child was snatched up to God and to his throne. The woman fled into the desert to a place prepared for her by God, where she might be taken care of for 1,260 days.
>
> And there was war in heaven. Michael and his angels fought against the dragon, and the dragon and his angels fought back. But he was not strong enough, and they lost their place in heaven (12:1-8).
>
> When the dragon saw that he had been hurled to the earth, he pursued the woman who had given birth to the male child. The woman was given the two wings of a great eagle, so that she might fly to the place prepared for her in the desert, where she would be taken care of for a time, times and half a time, out of the serpent's reach. Then from his mouth the serpent spewed water like a river, to overtake the woman and sweep her away with the torrent. But the earth helped the woman by opening its mouth and swallowing the river that the dragon had spewed out of his mouth. Then the dragon was enraged at the woman and went off to make war against the rest of her offspring – those who obey God's commandments and hold to the testimony of Jesus (vv. 13-17).

I know this reads like a science fiction thriller, so let's take a closer look at what God is revealing to us about the spiritual realm.

The first sign we see in the sun-clothed woman is national Israel and her son Jesus, the Messiah. The devil tried to kill Him when King Herod gave the decree to execute all the boys in Bethlehem two years old and younger (Matthew 2:3,16). But God protected Jesus.

The male child in John's vision is snatched up to God; this depicts Jesus' ascension to heaven after His resurrection. The devil is described as the "great red dragon."

In the Old Testament the wicked dragon represented the enemies of God and the nation of Israel (Psalm 74:14; Isaiah 27:1; Ezekiel 29:3). The dragon's seven heads depict universal wisdom, and his 10 horns denote great power by which he controls political empires.

This truth is seen in the histories of such nations as ancient Rome, Nazi Germany, the former Soviet Union, and modern-day Iraq. All of these sought to destroy the people of God (see Daniel 7:7, 24; Revelation 13:1; 17:3).

The seven crowns on his heads signify the ruling force of evil and Satan's rejoicing over the terror he has unleashed on the world. The third part of the stars which fell with him from heaven are the angels that fell with Lucifer in his rebellion (Revelation 12:7–9; see also Isaiah 14:12; Luke 10:18).

The devil cannot touch the Messiah, so the Dragon turns on the woman and the rest of her offspring. Since the church was born out of Judaism, the woman is both Israel and the church. God protects the woman and her children.

Believers in Jesus, the children of the sun-clothed woman, is taken by God into the desert, a place of protection, in the same way that the prophet Elijah was taken into the desert when he predicted the famine over Israel. It is interesting that Elijah stayed in the desert three and a half years—1,260 days—the same amount of time the woman and her offspring are in the desert. The 1,260 days simply represent the fact that God will sovereignly protect His people.

Look at the protection of God promised in this vision. The woman was given great eagle's wings, just as Israel was given when she came out of Egypt, and later the Babylonian Captivity (see Exodus 19:4; Deuteronomy 32:11, 12; Isaiah 40:31).

The three and a half years, or 42 months, parallel the 42 stages of Israel's journey in the wilderness (Numbers 33).

Now here's the exciting part—just when it looked like the devil would devour the woman by spewing out a great river, the earth swallowed the river (see Revelation 12:16). God uses even the elements of creation to come to our aid.

The point of this vision is to assure us that we are out of the serpent's reach. What a fantastic thought—you and I are beyond the reach of the devil. We are living under a canopy of God's protection and grace.

John saw the Dragon thrown out of heaven and hurled to the earth. That's what Jesus told us about the fall of Lucifer: "I saw Satan fall like lightning from heaven" (Luke 10:18).

We don't know exactly when Lucifer lost his place in heaven, bringing the angels with him. All we know is that he did fall, and that his fury is great because he knows his time is short.

He directs his fury and his rage toward the people of God. This depicts in a graphic way the term *spiritual warfare*. Now for more good news.

A SONG TO BE
REMEMBERED

In the middle of this troubling vision, John hears singing. It's as though God knows when John has seen about all the negative visions he can take, so the Lord gives him a break. He gets a good dose of positive praise to lift his spirit. Here is a song to remember the next time you find yourself in the midst of a spiritual battle:

> Then I heard a loud voice in heaven say: "Now have come the salvation and the power and the kingdom of our God, and the authority of his Christ.
>
> For the accuser of our brothers, who accuses them before our God day and night, has been hurled down.
>
> They overcame him by the blood of the Lamb and by the word of their testimony; they did not love their lives so much as to shrink from death. Therefore rejoice, you heavens and you who dwell in them! (Revelation 12:10-12).

The song of heaven announces, first of all, the sovereignty of God and of Christ. Next, we are assured that the devil has been cast down, which means that he has lost all spiritual authority.

It is important to understand what this means for our lives. Jesus Christ has "all authority in heaven and on earth" (Matthew 28:18). Not partial authority, not limited authority—all authority! It follows logically, then, that the devil has no authority.

Further, Jesus has given His people spiritual authority:

> "I have given you authority to trample on snakes and scorpions and to overcome all the power of the enemy; nothing will harm you" (Luke 10:19).

The snakes and scorpions He is referring to are demons. You and I have power over all evil in and through the name of Jesus. When the devil rears his head and roars like a terrifying lion, remember that he is only making noise. You have been given authority in Christ to defeat all the power of the enemy! You can overcome temptation, trials and deception because "The one who is in you is greater than the one who is in the world" (1 John 4:4).

No wonder Paul burst forth in praise, saying, "We are more than conquerors through him who loved us" (Romans 8:37). This majestic song of victory teaches us how to be overcomers in the spiritual war that is being waged on earth.

We Overcome by the Blood of the Lamb

The blood spoken of here is the sacrificial blood of Christ at Calvary. Just as Israel came out of Egypt by the blood of the Passover lamb, Paul says, "Christ, our Passover lamb, has been sacrificed" (1 Corinthians 5:7). We have already seen the figure of Christ portrayed as the Lamb of God, when John was translated to heaven in a vision.

Everything we have in Christ is based on what He has done for us, not what we do for Him. That's the difference between a religion based on grace and one based on works.

The fact that the devil is referred to here as "the accuser of our brothers" (Revelation 12:10) means that the primary way we get attacked spiritually is through a sense of failure, shame and guilt. The only antidote to guilt is the blood of the Lamb which has cleansed us, purified us and washed our sins away.

The power of the Lamb's blood will cover your past; you can say, "There is now no condemnation for those who are in Christ Jesus" (Romans 8:1). This means no verdict of guilty.

Personally, I find this verse to be one of the most reassuring statements in the Bible. Deliverance from guilt, shame and condemnation is ours when we firmly believe that "in Christ" there is no condemnation.

We Overcome by the Word of Our Testimony

John speaks often of the believer's testimony. From the outset he tells us that he was exiled to Patmos "because of the word of God and the testimony of Jesus" (1:9). When he sees the souls of the martyrs, he tells us that they were killed for their testimony (6:9). When the Dragon turns on the offspring of the woman we are considering in this chapter, notice that we are described as those who hold to the testimony of Jesus.

What is the overcomer's testimony? Our testimony is, first and foremost, about Jesus Christ. John writes in his First Epistle:

> That which was from the beginning, which we have heard, which we have seen with our eyes, which we have looked at and our hands have touched – this we proclaim concerning the Word of life. The life appeared; we have seen it and testify to it, and we proclaim to you the eternal life, which was with the Father and has appeared to us (1 John 1:1, 2).

When the Bible says that we overcome by the word of our testimony, it means that the most powerful testimony we can give the world is the testimony of Jesus Christ, the Son of God. Early Christians maintained a simple, yet powerful, testimony to the world about Jesus. We must do the same.

✝ Jesus Christ is the *Son of God* — divine, sinless and eternal.

✝ Jesus Christ is the *Messiah* sent by God to save us from our sins.

✝ Jesus Christ is *Lord*, with all power in heaven and on earth.

Perhaps the single most important question asked by our culture today is, Why does a 21st–century world need a first century Christ? After all, ours is the day of the knowledge explosion, the information superhighway, and the technological revolution.

Our culture is bombarded with a variety of new religions and self-help therapies. Is Jesus Christ really that unique among the spiritual and philosophical personalities of our day? This question strikes at the heart of the relevancy of the gospel. People are asking, Is Christ relevant to me? Does He have anything to say to my life?

The fact is, things are not as well as they seem. In spite of our self-made religions and technological achievements, the human experiment to build a utopian society has failed again. The experiment of the Tower of Babel has ended again in confusion. In the words of Augustine, we have attempted to build the city of man without the city of God. As a result, we experience a deep, inner void lacking the presence of God.

Only Jesus can fill the spiritual emptiness in our souls. The eternal Christ still speaks to every person and says, "I am the way, the truth and the life. No one comes to the Father except through me."

I like the way Thomas Aquinas explains this claim of Jesus:

> Without the way, no journey can be taken. Without the truth, no truth can be known. Without the life, no life can be lived. "I am the Way which must be followed; I am the Truth which must be believed; I am the Life for which man must hope."

Jesus Christ is the unique Son of God. He is fully God and fully man — the God-man. This is the greatest of all mysteries. The cornerstone of our faith is an understanding of who Jesus really is.

Paul majestically proclaimed, "Beyond all question, the mystery of godliness is great: He appeared in a body, was vindicated by the Spirit, was seen by angels, was preached among the nations, was believed on in the world, was taken up in glory" (1 Timothy 3:16).

✝ As man, He was born of a virgin; as God, He is from everlasting to everlasting.

✝ As man, He was wrapped in swaddling cloths and laid in a manger; as God, He spoke worlds into existence.

✝ As man, He walked the streets of Nazareth; as God, He walked on the water while the winds and the waves obeyed His voice.

✝ As man, He was hungry; as God, He said, "I am the bread of life."

✝ As man, He was thirsty; as God, He said, "I will give you living water to drink and you will never thirst again."

✝ As man, He was tired; as God, He said, "Come to me, all you who are weary and I will give you rest."

✝ As man, He was tempted; but as God, He knew no sin.

✝ As man, He prayed; as God, He answered prayer.

✝ As man, He was rejected, beaten and crucified; as God, He arose triumphant over the power of death, hell and the grave.

✝ As man, He was given a crown of thorns ; as God, He will return with clouds of heaven. Every knee will bow and every tongue confess that Jesus Christ is Lord!

Jesus Christ himself—in all of His power and glory, His truth and beauty, His divinity and humanity—is the word of our testimony by which we overcome sin, darkness and negativism in the world.

But our testimony must take on a personal note in order to have its fullest impact. It is one thing to merely confess who Jesus is, but quite another to share who He is in your own life.

Every person has to confront the Jesus question: Who is Jesus, and what will you do with Him? An anonymous writer puts it eloquently in "One Solitary Life":

> He was born in an obscure village. He worked in a carpenter's shop until He was 30. He then became an itinerant preacher. He never went to college. He never had a family or owned a house. He never held an office. He had no credentials but Himself.
>
> When He was only 33, the tide of public opinion turned against Him. All His friends ran away. He was handed over to his enemies and went through the mockery of a trial. He was nailed to a cross between two thieves. While He was dying, His executioners gambled for His clothing, the only possession He had on earth. He was laid in a borrowed grave.
>
> Nearly 20 centuries have come and gone, yet He remains the central figure of the human race. All the armies that ever marched, all the navies that ever sailed, all the parliaments that ever sat, and all the kings that ever reigned have not affected the life of man on this earth as much as this one solitary life.

The greatest evidence of the resurrection of Jesus Christ is the personal testimony of those who have met Him, and whose lives have been changed. The testimony that overcomes the devil is your personal testimony.

Every time you share your personal testimony with others, you overcome the powers of evil by letting your light shine in a world of darkness. The message of Revelation to the people of God is, "Speak up!"

The importance of our testimony is stressed in the statement made by a Protestant Christian in Nazi Germany during World War II:

> First they came for the Communists, I was not a Communist, so I said nothing. Then they came for the Jews. I was not a Jew, so I said nothing. Then they came for the Trade Unionists. I was not a Unionist, so I said nothing. Then they came for the Catholics. I was not a Catholic, so I said nothing. Last of all they came for me; and there was no one left to speak for me.

Whenever and wherever you speak out, your life validates your testimony. Testimony is not only spoken — it is lived. William Barclay challenges us: "The Christian dare not say, 'I care not what men say or think of me.' He must care, for his life is a testimony for or against his faith."

We Overcome by Courageous Commitment

Now, there is one final quality of the overcoming life we need to consider. John tells us, "They did not love their lives so much as to shrink from death" (Revelation 12:11). Obviously, he is thinking about those who have been willing to make the ultimate witness for Jesus by giving their lives for the gospel.

The history of the church is stained with the blood of the saints. More martyrs may have to make the ultimate sacrifice. But the real challenge in the Book of Revelation isn't to die for the gospel; it is to live for Christ. If any have to lay down their lives in martyrdom, God will give sufficient grace for that hour. But we lay our lives down for the gospel every day we live. The overcoming life is a selfless life of loving surrender for the cause of Christ and for the good of others. It's a life of courageous commitment to Jesus Christ, regardless of the cost.

Be honest: Can any of us who have been so richly blessed even talk about sacrifice? David Livingstone, one of the earliest missionaries to Africa, helps put things in perspective. In his article "The Call to Be a Missionary," he wrote:

> For my own part, I have never ceased to rejoice that God has appointed me to such an office. People talk of the sacrifice I have made in spending so much of my life in Africa. Can that be called a sacrifice which is simply paid back as a small part of a great debt owing to our God, which we can never repay? Is that a sacrifice which brings its own best reward in healthful activity, the consciousness of doing good, peace of mind, and the bright hope of a glorious destiny hereafter?

> Away with such a word, in such a view, and with such a thought! It is emphatically no sacrifice. Say, rather, that it is a privilege. Anxiety, sickness, suffering or danger, now and then, with a foregoing of the common convenience and charities of this life, may make us pause and cause the spirit to waver and sink; but let this only be for a moment!

> All of these are nothing when compared with the glory which will hereafter be revealed in and for us. I never made a sacrifice. Of this we ought not to talk, when we remember the great sacrifice made by Him who left His Father's throne on high to give Himself for us. "I am the way, the truth and the life" (John 14:6). Without the way there is no going; without the truth there is no knowing; Without the life there is no living."

No matter what we give, God always gives us more in return. It's true—you cannot outgive God. After Jesus instructed a wealthy young man about giving what he possessed to the poor, Peter boasted, "We have left all we had to follow you!"

Jesus responded, "No one who has left home or wife or brothers or parents or children for the sake of the kingdom of God will fail to receive many times as much in this age and, in the age to come, eternal life" (Luke 18:28-30). True Christianity can be costly, but the dividends are out of this world!

Overcomers never consider the cost of discipleship too high because they know God gives a hundredfold return. This letter written by Cyprian, the third-century bishop of Carthage, to his friend Donatus, an official in the Roman government, says it well:

> It's a bad world, Donatus, an incredibly bad world. But I have discovered in the midst of it a quiet and good people who have learned the secret of life. They have a joy and a wisdom which is a thousand times better than any of the pleasures of our sinful lives. They are despised and persecuted, but they care not. They are master of their own souls. They have overcome the world. These people, Donatus, are Christians, and I am one of them.

The Book of Revelation calls us heavenward. It asks us to measure this momentary life in light of eternal rewards.

Are your affections set on things above or on earthly things?

Are you looking to the temporary pleasures, peak experiences, and possessions of this life to bring you happiness?

Have you learned the secret of true happiness and prosperity: "Seek first his kingdom and his righteousness, and all these things will be given to you as well" (Matthew 6:33).

On the way to his execution in 1683, Sir William Russell, the English patriot, took a watch out of his pocket and handed it to the physician who was attending him.

"Would you kindly take my timepiece?" he asked. "I have no use for it. I am now dealing with eternity."

The Book of Revelation prepares us to face the reality of eternity.

Only when we can face eternity right are we ready to face life today.

Chapter
5

All pains the immortal spirit
must endure,
All weakness which impairs, all
griefs which bow,
Find their sole speech in that
victorious brow.

—Matthew Arnold in *Sohrab and Rustum*

A CALL FOR PATIENT ENDURANCE

If anyone is to go into captivity, into captivity he will go. If anyone is to be killed with the sword, with the sword he will be killed. This calls for patient endurance and faithfulness on the part of the saints (Revelation 13:10).

Perhaps the most mysterious personality in the Bible is the Antichrist. For many centuries, people have been intrigued by the idea of the Antichrist, curious about his identity, and terrified by the prospects of his emergence. Even Hollywood has produced such movies as *The Omen* and *The Seventh Sign,* to give their version of the Antichrist's coming. He has been identified as Nero, Adolph Hitler, and other dictatorial leaders down through the ages of church history.

Who is the Antichrist? The Bible calls him a worldwide ruler bent on global conquest. He will step onto the stage of human history at the beginning of the Great Tribulation (Matthew 24:21), which will last for seven years (Daniel 9:24-27).

He is the antithesis of Jesus Christ. He acts under the control of Satan, who leads the whole world astray. He is described by many terms in the Bible: the king of fierce countenance, the prince that shall come, the little horn, the king of the north, the man of sin, the lawless one, the son of perdition, and the beast out of the sea.

What will the Antichrist do when he comes on the scene? First, he will establish a peace treaty with Israel, promising that nation protection and prosperity.

During the Great Tribulation, he will violate that covenant, turn against Israel, and take the nation by force in the same way many of the Arab nations have attempted to do since the nation was reestablished in 1948.

He will persecute and martyr the righteous. He will change times and seasons. He will cause the world to worship Satan. He will blaspheme God. He will exert power over the world, and seek to be worshiped as though he himself were God.

Let's look closer at the role the Antichrist will play in the last days.

PORTRAIT OF
THE ANTICHRIST

In the Book of Revelation we see an unholy trinity consisting of Satan, the Antichrist and the False Prophet who terrorize the world during the Great Tribulation.

John watches anxiously as he sees the Antichrist rise up out of the sea of troubled humanity in his apocalyptic vision. This is what he saw:

> *And the dragon stood on the shore of the sea. And I saw a beast coming out of the sea. He had ten horns and seven heads, with ten crowns on his horns, and on each head a blasphemous name. The beast I saw resembled a leopard, but had feet like those of a bear and a mouth like that of a lion. The dragon gave the beast his power and his throne and great authority. One of the heads of the beast seemed to have had a fatal wound, but the fatal wound had been healed. The whole world was astonished and followed the beast. Men worshiped the dragon because he had given authority to the beast, and they also worshiped the beast and asked, "Who is like the beast? Who can make war against him?"*
>
> *The beast was given a mouth to utter proud words and blasphemies and to exercise his authority for forty-two months. He opened his mouth to blaspheme God, and to slander his name and his dwelling place and those who live in heaven. He was given power to make war against the saints and to conquer them. And he was given authority over every tribe, people, language and nation. All inhabitants of the earth will worship the beast — all whose names have not been written in the book of life belonging to the Lamb that was slain from the creation of the world* (13:1–8).

What kind of person will the Antichrist be? What will his personality be like? Remember that the Bible uses the term *antichrist* to refer to both a spirit force in the world today and an actual person who will rise to political position with global influence during the Great Tribulation (see 1 John 2:18, 22; 4:3; 2 John 7; Daniel 7:2-7; 2 Thessalonians 2:1-12).

John's vision gives us important insights into his personality. The Antichrist rises as a beast out of the sea. The sea represents the restless state of humanity that is due to political upheaval (Revelation 17:15). This imagery parallels Daniel's vision of the coming Gentile world powers which he saw emerge from the sea (Daniel 7:2–7).

John notices, first of all, that Antichrist has seven heads and 10 horns, with crowns on the horns. Let's sort out this strange symbolism.

The seven heads probably represent seven evil empires which have persecuted the covenant people of God, both Israel and the church. Six evil empires of history have openly warred against God. They include Egypt, Assyria, Babylon, Medo-Persia, Greece and Rome. The seventh is the Antichrist kingdom to come.

In general, the seven heads represent all anti-Christian empires throughout history and, in particular, these which have sought to destroy the church. Some see a parallel between the seven heads and the seven hills of ancient Rome which will form the capital of the Antichrist's empire.

His kingdom will certainly reflect the immorality of ancient Rome and the quest of the Caesars' bent for world conquest and emperor worship. Notice that on each head a blasphemous name was written. Paul foresaw the same diabolical nature of the Antichrist:

> Don't let anyone deceive you in any way, for that day [the coming of Christ] will not come until the rebellion occurs and the man of lawlessness is revealed, the man doomed to destruction. He will oppose and will exalt himself over everything that is called God or is worshiped, so that he sets himself up in God's temple, proclaiming himself to be God (2 Thessalonians 2:3, 4).

> For the secret power of lawlessness is already at work; but the one who now holds it back will continue to do so till he is taken out of the way [the Spirit-empowered church]. And then the

lawless one will be revealed, whom the Lord Jesus will over-
throw with the breath of his mouth and destroy by the splendor
of his coming. The coming of the lawless one will be in accor-
dance with the work of Satan displayed in all kinds of counter-
feit miracles, signs and wonders, and in every sort of evil that
deceives those who are perishing. They perish because they
refused to love the truth and so be saved (vv. 7–10).

Like the Dragon, the Antichrist has 10 horns, representing his vast political power. The 10 horns are the same as
the 10 toes and 10 horns Daniel saw in his visions (Daniel
2:40–45; 7:7, 8, 19–24). Some scholars believe that the 10
horns depict a literal 10-nation confederacy consisting of a
revived Roman empire.

The crowns on the heads speak of his rulership. The 10
horns indicate that he derives his power and position from
the Dragon, Satan himself. The awesome power of his global influence during the Tribulation is described in a fascinating way (Revelation 13:2, 3).

Borrowing again from the vision of Daniel, John says the
Antichrist kingdom will be like a leopard, reminiscent of
ancient Greece under Alexander the Great, who was swift
in his conquest.

He will resemble the bear, representing the Medo-Persian
empire under Cyrus the Great, which, with sheer size and
military might, conquered the impregnable city of Babylon.
The Antichrist kingdom will also resemble the lion, a symbol
of ancient Babylon under Nebuchadnezzar, who built the greatest city of the ancient world, filled with regal splendor.

Combined, this symbolism simply means that the Antichrist kingdom will be a combination of all the evil empires
that have existed throughout history. The Dragon will give
the Antichrist his power, his throne and his great authority

so that he will have political dominance in the global family of nations.

Notice something fascinating. John sees the Antichrist wounded, yet healed, almost miraculously. Perhaps this means that Antichrist will recover from a political or military attack that threatens to topple his empire. The tragic result is that the whole world will be astonished by his recovery and follow the Beast.

Whatever else could be said about this ruler to come, he will be a persuasive figure, to say the least. His whole purpose of existence will be to serve the interests of the Dragon. The Antichrist is merely a spiritual pawn in the hand of the Dragon.

The Revelator tells us that the world will worship the Dragon. The good news is that his days are numbered!

John's use of a time frame of 42 months, or 1,260 days, affirms the fact that the activity of the Antichrist will be limited by the sovereign rule of God. He is allowed only 42 months to blaspheme God and to persecute the people of God. Note carefully that this time period is the same as the time God protects His people from the Dragon in Revelation 12:6, 14—a period also called "a time, times and half a time."

While some like to spend time arguing about whether this time period describing the second half of the Great Tribulation is a literal three and a half years, one thing is certain: The time period tells us in no uncertain terms that God has limited the time the devil will be free to roam this earth and the Antichrist will be permitted to rule in terror.

Their days are numbered, and the victory of the people of God is sure!

ENTER THE
FALSE PROPHET

The Antichrist will not be alone. Among his entourage will be a man identified in the Revelation as the False Prophet.

While we seem to be getting more used to the idea of prophets these days, the downside of all this spiritual hype is that more and more people are duped by false prophecy. People are running after all kinds of prophets to give them some message of assurance, or a promise about their future.

Let's review what the Bible teaches about the authentic gift of prophecy that comes from God. Prophecy constitutes one of the most important ministries in the church.

The word *prophecy* simply means to tell forth the mind and heart of God. Biblical prophecy is motivated by the Holy Spirit of God. While it does not mean primarily to foretell the future, it can contain a predictive element. Prophecy has been described as a "springing forth" as a mighty stream, or a "dropping down" like honey from a full comb.

The Bible mentions 78 different prophets and prophetesses. A popular, but erroneous, concept of a prophet is one who only predicts the future. This definition falls short of true prophetic ministry.

The English word *prophet* is derived from the Greek word, *prophetes*, meaning "one who speaks for another." To the ancient Greeks this meant one who spoke for the gods.

The Hebrew word *nabi,* translated "prophet," means one who communicates (literally "pours forth") the will of God. The Old Testament prophets were God's representative speaking on His behalf to communicate the divine will and purpose of God to the people.

In interpreting and communicating the divine will, a prophet might deal with the past, present or future. The prophets' primary ministry was *forthtelling,* not *foretelling.* However, when prophets foretold the future, they did so only as it clarified God's plan of redemption and His ministry to Israel, other nations, or individuals.

Prophets announced the severe consequences of Israel's disobedience, as well as the blessings of their obedience, that would come to pass at some future date. Prophets always viewed Yahweh as the God of history, and proclaimed His sovereignty over all nations.

Today, we find ourselves living in the fulfillment of Jesus' prophecy concerning the last days:

> *"Watch out that no one deceives you. For many will come in my name, claiming, 'I am the Christ,' and will deceive many. And many false prophets will appear and deceive many people. . . . For false Christs and false prophets will appear and perform great signs and miracles to deceive even the elect – if that were possible"* (Matthew 24:4, 5, 11, 24).

Three times He warned that false prophets will come in the last days and deceive the masses. So great will be the spiritual deception of end times that even the elect would be deceived, if that were possible.

The spirit of false prophecy seen in the vast spread of false religions, cultic worship, and occultic practices sets the stage for the Antichrist and the greatest deception the world has ever seen.

The False Prophet will help champion the cause of the Antichrist during the Great Tribulation.

What role will the False Prophet play in the Antichrist kingdom?

> *Then I saw another beast, coming out of the earth. He had two horns like a lamb, but he spoke like a dragon. He exercised all the authority of the first beast on his behalf, and made the earth and its inhabitants worship the first beast, whose fatal wound had been healed. And he performed great and miraculous signs, even causing fire to come down from heaven to earth in full view of men. Because of the signs he was given power to do on behalf of the first beast, he deceived the inhabitants of the earth. He ordered them to set up an image in honor of the beast who was wounded by the sword and yet lived. He was given power to give breath to the image of the first beast, so that it could speak and cause all who refused to worship the image to be killed* (Revelation 13:11–15)

John sees the False Prophet rise as a beast out of the earth. He has two horns like a lamb, which means he has less power than the Antichrist and he is deceptively gentle.

He will speak like a Dragon, which tells us that all his prophecies will be inspired by the devil himself. This False Prophet represents the spirit of false religion, allied with state power which seeks to destroy the church (see 16:13; 19:20; 20:10).

What is his purpose? To represent and serve the Antichrist.

He will force people to worship the Beast by setting up an image of the Antichrist.

He will entice the world to submit to the agenda of the Antichrist by performing counterfeit miracles, and even calling down fire from heaven like Elijah of the Old Testament.

Most terrifying is his ruthlessness as he is shown killing those who refuse to worship the image of the Beast.

THE NUMBER
6 6 6

Now we come to the most popularized and intriguing symbol in the Revelation—the mark of the Beast, or 666. Here's what John saw in his vision:

> He also forced everyone, small and great, rich and poor, free and slave, to receive a mark on his right hand or on his forehead, so that no one could buy or sell unless he had the mark, which is the name of the beast or the number of his name.
>
> This calls for wisdom. If anyone has insight, let him calculate the number of the beast, for it is man's number. His number is 666 (13:16-18).

To understand the meaning of the mark of the Beast, we need to remember how marks were used in ancient times. Slaves were marked with the seal of the owner. The mark of the Beast identifies his followers as his property.

A mark was also used as a sign of allegiance. Ancient soldiers often branded themselves with the name of their commander. A mark was used in the drafting of a covenant. Documents, such as the certificates of Caesar issued in the first century, were sealed in ancient times.

So, the mark of the Beast identifies those who bear it as the followers of the Antichrist. But there is more to this mark: there is an economic consideration. The mark is a permit allowing people to conduct commerce, to buy and to sell, and to transact business. Those without the mark are said to be unable to buy or sell. They would have to buy what they need through underground sources.

The mark, then, represents economic persecution that has been enforced against the people of God down through the ages. Even today, Christians around the world in certain oppressive governments cannot buy or sell because of their Christian faith. When the Great Tribulation comes and the Antichrist rises to power, this mark may take the form of a global economy, and possibly a universal computer tracking every person alive. Technology indicates that not only is such a system possible, but inevitable.

Of all that the mark means, it is a mark of identification with the Antichrist. The mysterious number, 666, is the number of man in the sense that it falls short of seven, the number of God and perfection.

Since the Revelation is a book that often gives us contrasting symbols, we can't help but see the obvious contrast between the mark of the Beast, with which his followers are sealed, and the seal of God on the people of God (7:3).

The seal of God protects us from the wrath and judgment to come. While we can certainly differ in our opinions about what the mark of the Beast means in terms of the forecast of a global economy, there is no disputing the spiritual meaning of this mark.

The good news is that no one has to have the mark of the Beast — not today, not ever. You can be sealed with the Holy Spirit. The seal of God signifies that Christ's work of salvation is complete in your life. You belong to Him. Christ and God's proof of ownership is stamped forever on your life.

While the followers of the Beast bear his mark, the followers of Jesus bear the seal of the Holy Spirit:

> And you also were included in Christ when you heard the word of truth, the gospel of your salvation. Having believed, you were marked in him with a seal, the promised Holy Spirit, who is a deposit guaranteeing our inheritance (Ephesians 1:13, 14).

Unfortunately, more people seem curious and concerned about the mark of the Beast than are rejoicing that they are sealed with the Holy Spirit. My encouragement to you is to rejoice that you bear the seal of God, and that you belong to Him.

What I like most about the Revelation is that God always shows us the final score of the game. There is no suspense about how human history will end, or the final outcome of the Antichrist empire. The Antichrist and the False Prophet will meet their final doom in the lake of fire when Jesus returns at the Battle of Armageddon (19:19, 20).

But all of this seems so far in the future. What about now? Well, now we have to face the spirit of antichrist in the world that will one day set the stage for the actual Antichrist to rise on the scene.

SPIRIT OF THE
ANTICHRIST

Tucked away in the midst of these great and mysterious visions of the Antichrist—the beast out of the sea, the False Prophet, the beast out of the earth, and the mark of the Beast, 666—is a timeless message we desperately need today: "This calls for patient endurance and faithfulness on the part of the saints" (13:10).

Although the Antichrist and the False Prophet have yet to appear on the scene of human history, John tells us clearly:

> *Dear children, this is the last hour; and as you have heard that the antichrist is coming, even now many antichrists have come. This is how we know it is the last hour. . . . This is the spirit of the antichrist, which you have heard is coming and even now is already in the world* (1 John 2:18; 4:3).

Note his message: *The spirit of antichrist is already in the world.* We need to give serious attention to the implications of these words. Every day we live, we confront the spiritual pressure that the spirit of antichrist exerts against our minds, our families, our churches, our institutions and our government. It is a spirit of immorality, skepticism, rebellion and idolatry. In a word, it opposes all that is like God and Christ.

In the midst of what Paul so aptly labeled "a crooked and depraved generation" (Philippians 2:15), we are called to a life of patient endurance and faithfulness. This means we are to hold firmly to the faith and convictions of truth we have in Christ and in the Word of God.

Too many people are forsaking the time-tested values of the Word of God for the secular values of the day. As followers of Jesus, we live by a higher moral standard, the law of God. This is the only antidote to the antichrist spirit.

✝ When the world says that man is the measure of all things and God is simply the figment of your imagination, hold on to the first commandment, "You shall have no other gods before Me."

✝ When the world tempts you to worship the idols of power, pleasure, position and possessions, hold on to the second commandment, "You shall not make for yourselves any graven images."

✝ When the world slanders the name of God as though His name has no power or place in our hearts, or when it says to make vows in the name of God but don't worry if you break them, hold on to the third commandment, "You shall not take the name of the Lord your God in vain."

✝ When the world says to live in the fast lane and work without rest or worship so that you can succeed, hold

135

on to the fourth commandment, "Remember the Sabbath day and keep it holy."

✝ When the world tells you to show no respect for those in authority, beginning at home, or to rebel and go your own way, hold on to the fifth commandment, "Honor your father and mother."

✝ When the world says to express your anger, to practice violence and to hate your brother, hold on to the sixth commandment, "You shall not murder."

✝ When the world says to indulge the appetites of your carnal nature, to break your marriage vows, and to participate in the immoral lifestyle of the day, hold on to the seventh commandment, "You shall not commit adultery."

✝ When the world says to take advantage of your employer or employees, to look out for number one and deceive others so that you can make it to the top, hold on to the eighth commandment, "You shall not steal."

✝ When the world says to lie, to play games, to act the hypocrite and slander others, simply hold on to the ninth commandment, "You shall not bear false witness against your neighbor."

✝ When the world says that money is the answer for everything and the only way to be happy is to get more than you have, hold on to the tenth commandment, "You shall not covet."

No wonder Jesus challenges us in Revelation 3:11, "Hold on to what you have, so that no one will take your crown." The message is clear: "This calls for patient endurance and faithfulness on the part of the saints."

Winston Churchill was invited to deliver the commencement address at his alma mater, Harrow School. The auditorium was hot and the program tedious. When introduced, he approached the lectern and delivered a 29-word speech: "Never give in, never give in, never, never, never, never. In nothing great or small, large or petty, never give in, except to convictions of honor and good sense."

I was moved deeply as I read recently the testimony of Christians in China who have suffered greatly for the faith. Yet, in the midst of their suffering they report "miracles of endurance." Now there's a new twist on miracles. According to an article in *Charisma* magazine:

> During Chairman Mao's 10-year era of ideological madness, pastors were jailed, churches closed and all Bibles burned. Yet the church only grew through its endurance, proving Mao's fire to be a refining instead of a consuming force.
>
> "Endurance," says a Shanghai house-church leader, "is the 'Gethsemane gift.' It involves receiving the supernatural strength to continue glorifying God even though you would rather just die."
>
> Chinese believers regard this strength as supernatural, just like any miracle of healing. And so it was for Moses Xi, a Christian from Henan Province in eastern China. His strength proved to be miraculous for those he encountered, as well as for himself.
>
> Moses Xi was put into prison in 1995 for refusing to register his house church with the authorities. But he was terribly afraid in prison.
>
> "They did not sentence me but simply put me in prison," Moses says. "I thought I might be there for many years."
>
> On Moses' first night in prison, the guards decided to soften him up by sending three violent criminals into the 12-foot-square cell that Moses and four other men shared.

Moses was badly beaten. He lost four teeth, and his ribs were cracked, making it painful even to breathe.

The three men who beat Moses told him if he said nothing more about his Christianity, they would not harm him again. For the next month Moses was in anguish. He still was in excruciating pain from the beating, but he was in deeper turmoil over whether he should silence his witness and survive.

He prayed and prayed until he just decided to speak out again for Christ. Each time he did he was beaten. Twice he ended up in the prison infirmary, but for 18 months he endured and preached the gospel.

"Seventy-two prisoners accepted Jesus in that prison because God gave me strength to open my mouth," Moses says. He lost virtually all his teeth; a broken arm did not set properly; and he has a kidney disease caused by the sand that guards mixed into his daily ration of rice.[1]

The Revelation is not so much concerned with showing us the future as it is empowering us to live for Christ today with endurance and faithfulness. This is how we are to face the spirit of antichrist in the world today.

Michele Gold, in *Gratitude: A Way of Life*, tells about a father who gave his young daughter a simple locket and told her that it contained a valuable diamond sealed inside the locket; so if at any time she was ever in need, she could crack open the locket, sell the diamond, and make it through difficult times.

The daughter grew up and later struggled through tough financial times; but just the thought of the diamond resting safely around her neck gave her enough courage to pull through. Many years later she became successful and no longer struggled to survive. Her curiosity finally got the best of her, and she wanted to know how much the diamond was actually worth.

She took the diamond to a jeweler to have it appraised. She waited anxiously as he eyed the plain, tarnished locket with a bit of skepticism. She watched him raise his mallet, and with one swift blow, smash the little locket into many pieces. Inside was the small, smooth, clear stone.

The jeweler held it up to the light and said, "Why this isn't a diamond, my lady, it's a worthless piece of ordinary glass!"

Stunned by his words, the woman laughed. Then she cried. And then she laughed again.

"No sir," she said, "it is not worthless," as she wiped the tears from her eyes. "It is the most beautiful and valuable diamond in the world."

Her father had given her a priceless gem — the gift of hope, and the belief that you can make it regardless of the difficulties you face.[2]

Such is God's gift of the Revelation to us.

Chapter
6

What in me is dark
Illumine, what is low raise
and support;
That, to the height of this
great argument,
I may assert Eternal
Providence,
And justify the ways of God
to men.

—John Milton in *Paradise Lost*

144,000 SEALED

Then I looked, and there before me was the
Lamb, standing on Mount Zion, and with
him 144,000 who had his name and his
Father's name written on their foreheads
(Revelation 14:1).

The key to unlocking the spiritual riches of the Revela
tion is to understand the symbols and numbers in the
various visions. John uses symbolic language and numerology consistent with that of the Old Testament, especially the apocalyptic writings of Daniel, Ezekiel and
Zechariah.

Some scholars believe that symbolic language was used
for two main reasons: To maintain consistency of meaning
over the years of writing, and to encrypt the message so
that the persecutors of the people of God couldn't decode
the message. For example, Peter refers to the city of Rome
as Babylon in one of his letters.

The number seven is the most frequent number in the Bible, occurring 54 times in the Revelation. In the Book we see seven seals, seven trumpets, seven bowls of wrath and seven lampstands. Remember, seven represents completeness. God is portrayed as bringing His ultimate plan for creation to completion as seen in a new heaven and a new earth.

Of equal importance is the number 12 and its multiples, such as the 24 elders and the 144,000 who belong to God. Twelve, then, depicts people of God including both Old and New Testament believers.

This brings us to one of the most intriguing symbols of the Revelation, a mysterious group of people identified as the 144,000 witnesses in chapters 7 and 14. Who are they and what is their purpose?

First, let's clear up a terrible false teaching that has circulated in some groups on the fringe of Christianity: namely, that the 144,000 make up only those who are truly saved and go to heaven. This simply flies in the face of everything the Bible clearly teaches. Not only will more than 144,000 people go to heaven, the fact is that heaven is experiencing over-crowded conditions (7:9).

The number of people in heaven, then, is expansive rather than limited in scope. So, who are these 144,000? They represent two facets of the people of God: Jewish and Gentile believers. Together they form the covenant community just like the 24 elders we read about earlier. Since they are mentioned along with the 24 elders, the 144,000 may also speak specifically of a unique group of believers somewhat like the Messianic Jews.

The numerology of 144,000 is also used in John's description of New Jerusalem. The city is measured by an angel in

John's vision and found to be 12,000 stadia squared, with walls that are 144 cubits thick. The city has 12 gates bearing the names of the 12 tribes of Israel. It also has 12 foundations with the names of the 12 apostles.

This constant use of 12 and its multiples represent the complete community of faith that has existed down through the ages, both Jews and Gentiles. Paul the apostle tells us that God has brought Israel and the Church together in Christ:

> For he himself is our peace, who has made the two one and has destroyed the barrier, the dividing wall of hostility, by abolishing in his flesh the law with its commandments and regulations. His purpose was to create in himself one new man out of the two, thus making peace, and in this one body to reconcile both of them to God through the cross, by which he put to death their hostility. He came and preached peace to you who were far away and peace to those who were near. For through him we both have access to the Father by one Spirit.
>
> Consequently, you are no longer foreigners and aliens, but fellow citizens with God's people and members of God's household, built on the foundation of the apostles and prophets, with Christ Jesus himself as the chief cornerstone. In him the whole building is joined together and rises to become a holy temple in the Lord (Ephesians 2:14-21).

The first feature of the 144,000 that catches John's attention is the seal of God in their foreheads. What is this seal and how does it describe the people of God?

SEALED
BY GOD

The fact that the 144,00 are sealed tells us that God has a special plan for His people and that He watches over us.

The act of God sealing His people first appears in the Revelation when the sixth seal is opened (6:17).

Remember that when the sixth seal is opened cataclysmic judgments are unleashed on the earth. But in the midst of judgment the people of God are sealed for protection. John describes it this way:

> *After this I saw four angels standing at the four corners of the earth, holding back the four winds of the earth to prevent any wind from blowing on the land or on the sea or on any tree. Then I saw another angel coming up from the east, having the seal of the living God. He called out in a loud voice to the four angels who had been given power to harm the land and the sea: 'Do not harm the land or the sea or the trees until we put a seal on the foreheads of the servants of our God.' Then I heard the number of those who were sealed: 144,000 from all the tribes of Israel (7:1-4).*

The seal, then, assures us that we are protected by God. As Paul wrote, "Since we have now been justified by his blood, how much more shall we be saved from God's wrath through him!" (Romans 5:9). The good news is that "God did not appoint us to suffer wrath but to receive salvation through our Lord Jesus Christ" (1 Thessalonians 5:9).

When John sees a vision of judgment or the persecution of God's people in the Revelation, God always gives him a sequel vision of hope for the victorious church. As in the vision of the 144,000.

This seal is also a mark of identification. This is the case in Ezekiel's vision where the people are sealed to mark the true servants of God from the false (Ezekiel 9:4-7). The Revelation constantly gives us contrasting pictures. Here we see two distinct groups sealed: the followers of the beast and the followers of the Lamb.

Finally, the seal indicates security. Paul writes, "The foundation of God stands sure having this seal: 'The Lord knows those who are his,' " then he adds, 'Everyone who confesses the name of the Lord must turn away from wickedness'" (2 Timothy 2:19). Every believer is marked with this seal:

> *Now it is God who makes both us and you stand firm in Christ. He anointed us, set his seal of ownership on us, and put his Spirit in our hearts as a deposit, guaranteeing what is to come* (2 Corinthians 1:21, 22).

Early Christians considered water baptism to be a seal. We find the real meaning of the seal in Ephesians:

> *And you also were included in Christ when you heard the word of truth, the gospel of your salvation. Having believed, you were marked in him with a seal, the promised Holy Spirit. And do not grieve the Holy Spirit of God, with whom you were sealed for the day of redemption* (Ephesians 1:13; 4:30).

The seal has a three-fold meaning: *divine ownership, a finished transaction and divine protection.* Note that the seal on the 144,000 includes both the names of the Father and the Lamb, which means that they belong to both (14:1; 3:12).

We talk a lot today about the problems of low self-esteem, poor self-image and a lack of confidence. The answer to these negative feelings is the realization that you are sealed by God. You belong to Him. He has finished the work of salvation in your life. You are secure in Him.

When you realize what this seal really means in your life you will joyfully declare in the face of every challenge and circumstance, that "in all these things we are more than conquerors through him who loved us" (Romans 8:37).

Evangelist Peter Dyneka left his homeland in Russia as a

teenager on March 11, 1898. He sailed from Libau, Russia, bound for Halifax, Nova Scotia, on the *SS Dvinsk,* a Russian liner. For 14 days and nights the ship pushed its way through the stormy Atlantic.

Peter's mother had packed enough food for the whole voyage. The box was so large he had to have a friend help him carry it aboard. Every day he would walk past the dining room longing to eat the delicious meals prepared for the wealthy passengers. But because he was trying to save his money, he would go back to his room to eat his black bread and garlic.

Later, some of the sailors tricked Peter into doing their work in exchange for meals from the dining room. So he worked hard every day for the rest of his meals across the Atlantic. It wasn't until the last day of the voyage that he learned that three daily meals in the ship's dining room were included in the price of his ticket![1] The point is, You're richer than you think! You are sealed by God as His very own.

WHO ARE THE
CHOSEN PEOPLE?

Since the sealing of the 144,000 has allusions to both Israel and the Church, let's look at the seal from these two perspectives. The history of Israel is the story of the providence of God. Abraham is the father of the Hebrew nation. The word *Hebrew* is an English equivalent of the word *Habiru* meaning "wanderer" or "sojourner." It refers to the nomadic lifestyle of the patriarchs.

The later term *Jew* originally referred to those belonging to the tribe of Judah; but later it came to refer to anyone and everyone of the Hebrew race.

National Israel

The history of the Jewish people is one marked by the fingerprints of God. They have endured rejection, invasion, captivity and dispersion; yet they occupy center-stage in contemporary history. God's covenant to Abraham still stands:

> "I will make you into a great nation and I will bless you; I will make your name great, and you will be a blessing. I will bless those who bless you, and whoever curses you I will curse; and all peoples on earth will be blessed through you" (Genesis 12:2, 3).

During the reign of Russian Czar Peter the Great, an elderly preacher was imprisoned for his faith. The Czar summoned him and asked, "Can you give me one infallible proof to verify the Bible?" "Yes, Sire," he replied, "the Jew."

The Past. Jewish history is, in reality, the story of faith and the faithfulness of God. Their history can be traced along the following dateline:

2,000 B.C. Abraham is called from Ur of Chaldees to the Promised Land.

1,450 B.C. The Exodus is completed under the leadership of Moses.

1,400 B.C. Joshua leads the conquest of Canaan.

1,380 B.C. The period of the Judges lasts 330 years.

1,053 B.C. Saul is inaugurated as the first king of Israel.

1,013 B.C. The Davidic Kingdom is established and the covenant given.

930 B.C. Israel is divided after Solomon's death.

722 B.C. Israel (northern kingdom) is invaded by Assyria and exiled.

586 B.C. Judah (southern kingdom) is invaded by Babylon and exiled.

539 B.C. Jews return to Jerusalem after 70 years of Babylonian captivity.

165 B.C. Jews rededicate the temple after defeating the Syrians (Hanukkah).

63 B.C. Rome rises to power and controls Israel.

70 A.D. Rome, under Titus, destroys Jerusalem and temple (Masada).

135 A.D. Hadrian invades Israel and renames it Palestine.

1882 A.D. The first group of Jewish colonists in recent centuries settle in Palestine.

1914 A.D. England, France, and Russia declare war on the Ottoman Turks.

1917 A.D. Forces under General Allenby advance into Palestine.

1918 A.D. The Balfour Declaration is signed; the British guarantee a Jewish state.

1948 A.D. The United Nations recognizes Israel as an independent state.

1948 A.D. A War of Independence is fought against five Arab states.

1956 A.D. The Sinai Campaign is fought against Egypt, Jordan and Syria.

1967 A.D. The Six Day War results in the Jews recapturing Jerusalem.

1973 A.D. The Yom Kippur (Day of Atonement) War.

1995 A.D. A peace treaty is signed between Israel and Syria.

Throughout the Biblical period the Jewish religion developed through a series of stages including the Patriarchal Period (Genesis), the Mosaic Period and the Law, the Intertestamental Period, the Rabbinical Period (during Christ's time), the Medieval Period and the Modern Period.

The result today is a unified Jewish faith consisting of diverse sects, including *Orthodox* (strict adherence to law and tradition), *Reformed* (or Neo-Orthodox, a reaction to orthodoxy), *Conservative* (a blend of orthodox and reformed) and *Messianic* (those who accept Jesus as Israel's Messiah).

The Future. What does God have in store for Israel in the future? The Bible tells us in no uncertain terms that Israel will be saved and protected in the last days. That means that one day Israel will recognize Jesus as her long-awaited Messiah. Paul the apostle, himself a Jew, said:

> *I do not want you to be ignorant of this mystery, brothers, so that you may not be conceited: Israel has experienced a hardening in part until the full number of the Gentiles has come in. And so all Israel will be saved, as it is written: "The deliverer will come from Zion; he will turn godlessness away from Jacob"* (Romans 11:25, 26).

When Harry Truman was asked on one occasion what was his greatest contribution as President he responded, without hesitation, that it was to sign the United Nations Resolution recognizing Israel as an independent state.

Israel was birthed as a nation around 2,000 B.C. through the descendants of Abraham. Time and time again, it has survived invasion and exile. When it looked like the end was near, God has always raised up His people. The nation's ultimate national desolation came in A.D. 70 when Titus and the Roman army invaded and destroyed Jerusalem, as Jesus predicted in Matthew 24:1-3.

For 19 centuries the Holy Land lay desolate. Then, in the words of the prophets, the desert began to blossom like a rose. The fig tree that was barren began to bloom again in fulfillment of the prophecy of the Bible (see Amos 9:14, 15).

On May 15, 1948 the "Israel sign" of the last days began to be fulfilled. Since that date she has conquered her enemies in the four conflicts and wars waged against her. They are the 1948 War of Independence, the 1956 Sinai Campaign, the 1967 Six-Day War, and the 1973 Yom Kippur War.

A spiritual seal exists over Israel. God is raising the nation up in the last days to display His glory and to confirm to us that He is the God of providence. He watches over His word to perform it (Jeremiah 1:12).

Some see in this sign of the 144,000 a group of Messianic believers who will witness for Jesus as Messiah during the tribulation period. They will oppose the Antichrist, just as the Maccabean rebels opposed Antiochus Epiphanes in 168 to 165 B.C.

Spiritual Israel

When the Bible talks about Israel it is not merely speaking of national Israel. The descendants of Abraham include both those who are blood descendants and spiritual descendants — those who have put their faith in God and in Christ Jesus. This is the point Paul makes so poignantly to the Romans:

> *Therefore, the promise comes by faith, so that it may be by grace and may be guaranteed to all Abraham's offspring — not only to those who are of the law but also to those who are of the faith of Abraham. He is the father of us all. As it is written: ' I have made you a father of many nations'"* (Romans 4:16, 17).

The true Israel does not consist merely of those who are born of the human ancestry of Abraham. It also includes those who are born again through faith in Jesus Christ.

It is interesting to study the New Testament passages which compare Israel and the church. The identity of the New Testament church is rooted in the history of Israel in the plan of God. For example, believers in Christ are referred to as branches which have been grafted into Israel, the vine (Romans 11:17).

Old Testament prophets foretold God's inclusion of Gentiles into the covenant (see Hosea 1:10; 2:23). Paul goes on to tell us that Christ has destroyed the dividing wall between Jews and Gentiles, making out of the two one new man (Ephesians 2:11-18). The true Jew is one who is circumcised in his heart, not just in the flesh.

Not all who are descended from Israel in the flesh are Israel (see Romans 2:28, 29; 9:6). Believers in Jesus are children of Abraham and heirs of the promise (see Galatians 3:6-26). The church is addressed by the apostles as "the Israel of God" (Galatians 6:16), and "the twelve tribes scattered among the nations" (James 1:1). Just as Israel is referred to as "a nation of priests" (Exodus 19:6), the church is called a "royal priesthood, a holy nation" (1 Peter 2:9).

This does not mean that God has abandoned His plan for the nation of Israel; He has not. However, the covenant of Abraham promised a blessing for "all nations," and that certainly includes the Gentiles.

Our Christian forefathers were Jews. Christianity grew out of Judaism as the fulfillment of God's promises in the law and prophets. First century Jewish Christians first worshiped in synagogues. Christianity was simply regarded as a sect of Judaism called "the Way" (see Acts 9:2).

Christianity and Judaism parted company due to the persecution of Christians, launched initially by Saul of Tarsus. Later, Christianity became heavily identified with Gentiles who readily accepted the Gospel.

In many respects the commission of the church corresponds to God's call to Israel. God chose Israel to witness of the one true God in the midst of pagan worship (Deuteronomy 6:4, 5); to demonstrate the blessings of serving and obeying God (Psalms 144:15); to preserve the Word of God from generation to generation (Psalm 145:1-7); to prepare for the coming of the Messiah (Isaiah 40:1-3); to live a holy life in priestly ministry (Exodus 19:6; Leviticus 11:45); and to demonstrate the love of God for all nations (Genesis 12:1-3).

This is why we know that the symbol of the 144,000 includes everyone in the covenant of salvation, both Jewish and Gentile believers. Look at some fascinating facts about the list of the twelve tribes given in the account of the 144,000. They let us know that this is a spiritual symbol and not simply a literal counting of Jewish believers.

Two tribes are missing from the list!

> *From the tribe of Judah 12,000 were sealed, from the tribe of Reuben 12,000, from the tribe of Gad 12,000, from the tribe of Asher 12,000, from the tribe of Naphtali 12,000, from the tribe of Manasseh 12,000, from the tribe of Simeon 12,000, from the tribe of Levi 12,000, from the tribe of Issachar 12,000, from the tribe of Zebulun 12,000, from the tribe of Joseph 12,000, from the tribe of Benjamin 12,000 (7:5-8).*

Notice first that the tribe of Dan is missing. This is because Dan fell prey to idolatry (see Judges 18:18, 19; 1 Kings 12:29, 30). Ephraim is missing because they were also idolatrous (Hosea 4:17).

Besides the two missing tribes, the birth order of the sons is altered. Because Judah is the royal or Messianic tribe, it is listed first (although Reuben was actually the firstborn son of Jacob). Jesus descended from the royal line of Judah, and as our Messiah He is given preeminence.

The point is that the list has a spiritual meaning; it is more than mathematics. You may also find it interesting to know that in the Old Testament the 12 tribes are listed in 18 different orders to illustrate various spiritual truths. John's list is unique as he seeks to show us the complete company of the redeemed of all ages—"those who follow the Lamb wherever He goes" (14:4).

MORE THAN
CONQUERORS

The relationship of the 144,000 to the Lamb clearly identifies them as believers. To understand their role in the plan of God, we need to see the majestic portrayal of the Lamb of God in John's vision.

Remember, John first saw Jesus as the Lamb slain before the throne of God, and all praise in heaven was given to Him. Once again, he sees the triumphant lamb of God, Jesus Christ.

Then I looked, and there before me was the Lamb, standing on Mount Zion, and with him 144,000 who had his name and his Father's name written on their foreheads. And I heard a sound from heaven like the roar of rushing waters and like a loud peal of thunder. The sound I heard was like that of harpists playing their harps. And they sang a new song before the throne and before the four living creatures and the elders. No one could learn the song except the 144,000 who had been redeemed from

*the earth. These are those who did not defile themselves with
women, for they kept themselves pure. They follow the Lamb
wherever he goes. They were purchased from among men and
offered as firstfruits to God and the Lamb. No lie was found in
their mouths; they are blameless* (14:1-5).

This victorious scene comes right on the heels of the dark,
foreboding vision of the Antichrist, the False Prophet and
the Mark of the Beast in chapter 13. I think I would be in
the mood for something positive after seeing all that, too!

He sees the Lamb of God in His triumphant glory and
splendor. With Him are the 144,000, standing on Mount
Zion, which, in the vision is heaven itself.

Historically, Mount Zion is the ancient Jebusite stronghold captured by David which later became Jerusalem (2
Samuel 5:7; Psalm 48:1-14). But Mount Zion is also the spiritual Jerusalem in heaven (see Hebrews 12:22-24; Galatians
6:4). As a stronghold, the symbol of Mount Zion reminds us
that God is our refuge and strength against the attacks of Satan himself.

Then we see and hear, as it were, the 144,000 playing
harps and singing. Heaven explodes with a holy symphony
of musical praise that sounds like the roar of rushing waters: the redeemed are singing "a new song." Songs are
important in Scripture.

Moses and Israel sang after the Red Sea opened (Exodus
15). Deborah sang after she led Israel in victory over Syria
(Judges 5). Judah sang, "Give thanks to the Lord for He is
good, His love endures forever" as they marched into battle
(2 Chronicles 20). David declared, "Sing to the Lord a new
song, play skillfully and shout for joy!" (Psalm 33:3).

Paul and Silas sang at midnight in a Philippian jail (Acts
16). More importantly, Jesus sang a hymn on his way to

Gethsemane and the cross, "This is the day the Lord has made, I will rejoice and be glad in it" (see Matthew 26:30).

But the greatest song of all is the "new song" of the redeemed who know the joy of sins forgiven. It's called a new song because it celebrates the new life we have in Christ. In Him we have received a new heart and a new spirit (Ezekiel 36:26, 27), a new mind (Romans 12:2), a new self (Ephesians 4:24), a new covenant (Matthew 26:28), a new name (2:17) and, one day, we will receive a new heaven and a new earth (21:1).

So let us join the host of heaven's redeemed and sing the new song in praise to Him who is seated on the throne and declares, "Behold, I make all things new!"

A NEW
LIFESTYLE

Spiritual worship involves more than singing; worship is a way of life that brings glory to God and to Christ. Such is the lifestyle of the 144,000.

A young man named Jim came into our church and accepted Christ into his life. He had just started on his journey with the Lord when he moved back home to New York.

After being there a few months he wrote me a letter explaining that he had met some Jewish friends and was learning about Judaism and the background of his Christian faith. He made a statement in his letter I'll never forget. He said, "I think I now understand the difference between Christianity and Judaism. Christianity is a way of believing and Judaism is a way of life."

Unfortunately, he had missed the point of the Christian life. But he did put his finger on a prevailing problem of our times, namely, that many people think of Christianity only in terms of what we believe, not how we live.

We know of course that true faith results in a changed life. What we believe and how we live go hand in hand. As Paul says, "We live by faith not by sight" (2 Corinthians 5:7). And James reminds us that "faith without works is dead" (James 2:17).

The 144,000 lived a life of purity. They did not defile themselves with women. This is not intended to be a sexist statement. It simply refers to a life of moral purity — what we call integrity. Purity comes to us as a gift from God when we confess our sins. But purity is also a lifestyle as we strive to "walk worthy of the Lord and please Him in every way" (Colossians 1:9). I especially like that verse and seek to live it out in my daily life.

A few years ago my son, David Paul, who was 10 years old at the time, said he wanted to program a screen saver on my PC. When he asked me what message I wanted, this verse came to my mind. To this day, when I turn on my computer these words scroll over and over on the screen: "Walk worthy of the Lord and please Him in every way."

They also lived a life of obedience to Christ. John says, "They follow the Lamb wherever he goes." That was the call Jesus gave to every person He met. "Follow me," He said.

When you hear the word *Christian*, what comes to your mind? Today the word is used so lightly and in such varied contexts that we are prone to ask, "Will the real Christians please stand up?"

In the New Testament, the word *Christian* appears only three times (Acts 11:26; 26:28; 1 Peter 4:16). It comes from two words: *Christ* and *man*. Christ living in a man . . . a man living in Christ — a dynamic relationship.

German theologian Adolf Deissman suggests that the word *Christian* means "slave of Christ" in the same way that the word *Caesarean* means "slave of Caesar." To be a Christian, then, is to be in relationship to Jesus Christ. That's what He meant when He said, "Come follow me."

We do not become Christians en mass as was attempted in Emperor Constantine's edict that the entire Roman army be baptized Christian, or when Emperor Theodosius I declared Christianity the state religion of Rome.

We are not Christians because of our nationality, moral convictions or family background. To be a Christian is a matter of personal faith in Jesus Christ. It is to be like Thomas who, when he met the Risen Lord, said, "My Lord and My God." The question of faith is the question posed by Pilate, "What then shall *I* do with Jesus who is called the Christ?" The Christian answers with assurance, "I know whom I have believed" (2 Timothy 1:12).

Sometimes we think of Christians as people who are perfect, or at least are trying to be perfect. Believe me, nothing could be further from the truth. We are forgiven, indeed; but far from perfect.

It reminds me of the minister whose five-year-old asked him, "Dad, what is a Christian?"

His father explained that Christians believe in Jesus, read their Bible, pray, love others, do what is right, control their tempers, are always kind. The little boy stopped him and said, "Dad, have I ever seen a Christian?"

All Jesus says is, "Follow me." To *follow* means to go in the same direction, to be a close companion, to surrender will to Him. Caleb followed the Lord fully (Numbers 14:34). David said, "My soul follows hard after you O God" (Psalm 63:8).

159

And the 144,000 follow the Lamb wherever He goes in un-reserved obedience. Wilson Carlisle, founder of the Christian Army, said, "Jesus captured my heart. For me to know Jesus is a love affair."

The 144,000 teach us to live a life of dedication to Christ. "They were purchased from among men and offered as firstfruits to God." The reference to *being purchased* simply means that we have been redeemed from our sins by the death of Jesus on the cross (see 1 Peter 1:18-20).

But what does the statement about *being firstfruits* mean? Such wording is difficult for us because we no longer live in the agricultural age; ours is the information age. The Bible often refers to God's people as His firstfruits (see Jeremiah 2:3; James 1:18; Romans 16:5; 1 Corinthians 15:20).

The firstfruit offering is the best of the crop—a sign of hope that the rest of the crop will come in. The firstfruits were offered to God as an expression that the entire harvest would be dedicated to God. In the same way Christians are to give their best for God. Our whole lives, regardless of our occupation or career, are to be dedicated to God for His service.

George Truett tells about a cattleman who attended one of his crusades in Texas. That morning he preached on dedication to God from 1 Corinthians 6:20, "You are not your own; you are bought with a price." The cattleman went to him after the service and asked him to visit his ranch that afternoon.

The cattleman had only been a Christian for a short time. They traveled up the canyon about a mile. The cattleman then showed Truett his vast ranch of a thousand acres. He said: "I didn't know until today that all of this is God's, not mine. Please pray for me as I dedicate myself and all that I own to God. From now on I will be His manager."

After Truett finished praying for him, the cattleman prayed a simple prayer: "And Lord, please bring my wayward son to know you." That night in the evening service, the cattleman's son came with his father to the service and gave his life to Jesus Christ.

As Nels Ferre, in *Christ and the Christian,* said, "The Church is the fellowship of the dead-to-themselves and the alive-for-Christ." That's the meaning of dedication.

Finally, the 144,000 model a life of integrity. "No lie was found in their mouths; they are blameless." The offerings of the old covenant were to be blameless, and this was a clear call for the worshiper who offered the sacrifice to live a blameless life.

The old prophet said, "The remnant of Israel will do no wrong; they will speak no lies, nor will deceit be found in their mouths. They will eat and lie down and no one will make them afraid" (Zephaniah 3:13). In the New Testament Paul tells us, "For he chose us in him before the creation of the world to be holy and blameless in his sight" (Ephesians 1:4).

Today, we use the word *integrity.* According to Webster, *integrity* means "uprightness of character; probity and honesty." It is the condition or quality of being sound or unimpaired; the state of being complete or undivided. In other words, we don't play the part of the hypocrite, like an actor on a stage. We possess congruity between what we believe and how we live, what we say and what we do.

Before becoming President, Theodore Roosevelt was a rancher out West. One day while he and some of his ranch hands were rounding up stray cattle, they happened to wander onto a neighbor's property where they found an unbranded calf.

By Western tradition, the calf belonged to the neighbor, but one of Roosevelt's cowboys started to put the Roosevelt brand on the calf.

Roosevelt asked why he was doing this and was told, "I always put on the boss's brand."

Roosevelt fired the man on the spot. "A man who will steal for me," he said, "will steal from me." *Integrity* means to be consistent in your convictions even when it costs you.

When we read this description of the 144,000 we are challenged to a higher standard of living. Such a grand view of the people of God calls us upward and onward! There's simply no way to think about the return of Jesus Christ and not have it affect the way we spend our time here on earth and the way we live out our days.

Dr. James M. Gray said that the hope of Christ's return made a five-fold impact on his life:

1. It awakened in him a real love and enthusiasm for the study of every part of God's word.

2. It quickened his zeal for Christian service, especially for world missions.

3 It delivered his mind from an overwhelming ambition for worldly success and the praise of men.

4. It developed patience and quietness in the face of unjust treatment.

5. It broke the bands of covetousness and set him free to give his possessions to the Lord.

As World War II was drawing to a close, C.S. Lewis, professor at Oxford, lectured to a group of students. He paused and asked the class, "How can you go to college and study literature when London is under siege?"

Then he answered his own question.

"We're always under siege," he said.

The same holds true for us today. The real question is, Will you spend your life dealing with the immediate, or dealing with eternal matters?

Chapter

7

Don't be embarrassed to speak up for our Master. . . . Take your share of the suffering for the Message along with the rest of us. We . . . only keep on going, after all, by the power of God, who first saved us and then called us to this holy work.

—2 Timothy 1:8, 9, TM

CALLED, CHOSEN AND FAITHFUL

They will make war against the Lamb, but the Lamb
will overcome them because he is Lord of lords and
King of kings — and with him will be his called,
chosen and faithful followers (Revelation 17:14).

Winston Churchill once said, "The farther back you look, the farther forward you are likely to see." The Book of Revelation possesses the amazing quality of reflecting on past history in order to reveal the future more fully.

This is certainly the case when John tells us about God's judgment on the great city he identifies as Mystery Babylon the Great. The old city of Babylon was the cradle of civilization in an ancient land known as Mesopotamia. The Bible tells us what happened at Babel, a name meaning "confusion." Here the Tower of Babel was built and the people organized themselves in rebellion against God.

Centuries later the Babylonian Empire became a dominant world power that ruthlessly took the Jews into captivity for a period of 70 years. Today, political tensions are constant in Iraq, the site of ancient Babylon.

The famous city of Babylon is located just south of Baghdad. It was built on the Euphrates River by King Nebuchadnezzar. His magnificent Hanging Gardens are regarded as one of the seven wonders of the ancient world. So, the figure of Babylon has a past, present and future meaning.

Why is so much attention given to the rise and fall of Babylon in the Revelation? Remember that this letter was originally sent to early Christians facing Roman persecution. As such, the Book of Revelation parades the triumph of Christ and His church across the stage of its drama.

Jesus is portrayed as the Lion of the tribe of Judah, who has conquered. The church is pictured as being victorious over Satan, the Antichrist and the False Prophet. God the Father is revealed as the One who will complete His eternal plan for the ages.

All of this was written to encourage early believers to be faithful even if it meant death. Many Christians have suffered since the birth of the church at Pentecost. Believers were enduring intense persecution when the Revelation was sent by the apostle John to the seven churches in Asia.

After the time of Nero and the great fire of Rome in A.D. 64 (Nero blamed it on the Christians), the church experienced untold persecution by the Roman government under despots such as Domitian. The consistent stand of our forefathers and foremothers overcame, in time, the oppression of Rome. Today, ancient Rome lies buried in the sands of time, but the church marches on. Why? Because the church is comprised of the called, the chosen and the faithful.

As the first century drew to a close, the church needed to be encouraged to remain faithful regardless of the cost. Nero had executed two of the most influential apostles in the church, Peter and Paul. Emperor Domitian had established the law of emperor worship, and Christians had refused to observe it. John, the last apostle, was now exiled on the island of Patmos — a Roman penal colony designated for the worst of criminals.

In A.D. 95, John received the Revelation while a prisoner on Patmos. After two years of exile, John was released under the order of Nerva, who repealed the laws of emperor worship. John wrote this book as an exile for his faith. He wrote to those who were facing the worst of what we call spiritual warfare — the reality of persecution that meant financial disaster, imprisonment and, for some, even death. He identifies himself with the suffering church from the very outset of the letter:

> I, John, your brother and companion in the suffering and kingdom and patient endurance that are ours in Jesus, was on the island of Patmos because of the word of God and the testimony of Jesus (1:9).

These early Christians were confused by the attacks on their faith. They wondered how God could allow such opposition to the gospel. To answer their concerns, the Holy Spirit pulled back the curtain and revealed the reality of spiritual warfare against the church in the form of five enemies. We have already seen them: the Dragon, the beast out of the sea; the Antichrist, the beast out of the earth; the False Prophet; the mark of the Beast, the economic persecution of believers; and Mystery Babylon the Great.

In the midst of it all, God promises that we will triumph over evil and will be brought into His eternal kingdom.

Throughout history God is faithful to judge evil and will one day render His final judgment against the world during the Great Tribulation.

This is the "mystery of God" which will be accomplished under the seventh trumpet judgment denoting the outpouring of the seven bowls of wrath (10:8). The "mystery of God" speaks of God's complete victory over evil.

The final "evil empire" of human history will be the Antichrist's kingdom. God will destroy it when He plunges the earth into darkness, as seen in the fifth bowl of wrath (16:10, 11). The Revelator is also careful to systematically reveal the defeat of our enemies:

† those who have the mark of the Beast (ch. 15);

† Mystery Babylon, the Antichrist and the False Prophet (chs. 17-19);

† the Dragon—Satan himself (ch. 20).

The bottom line of all this is that regardless of Satan's attacks against the redeemed people of God, the sure promise from Christ is: "Upon this rock I will build my church; and the gates of hell shall not prevail against it" (Matthew 16:18, KJV).

This is why believers are addressed as "overcomers" in the Revelation. The final promise is, "He who overcomes will inherit all this, and I will be his God and he will be my son" (21:7). The judgment of God against sin and the demise of Satan's kingdom are crucial components in the victory of God.

Thus, the Revelation has much to say about the final consummation of God's judgment, which ushers in the kingdom of Christ. From this point on, John shows us the judgment of God against the enemies of the church.

JUDGMENT DAY IS
A COMIN'

Before seeing the coming judgment, John's attention is once again drawn to the heavenly scene:

> *I saw in heaven another great and marvelous sign: seven angels with the seven last plagues — last, because with them God's wrath is completed. And I saw what looked like a sea of glass mixed with fire and, standing beside the sea, those who had been victorious over the beast and his image and over the number of his name. They held harps given them by God and sang the song of Moses the servant of God and the song of the Lamb:*
>
> *"Great and marvelous are your deeds, Lord God Almighty. Just and true are your ways, King of the ages. Who will not fear you, O Lord, and bring glory to your name? For you alone are holy. All nations will come and worship before you, for your righteous acts have been revealed"* (15:1-4).

This eternal perspective sustains John as he watches the unfolding drama of the judgment of God on evil. He sees a great and marvelous sign (the third such sign mentioned in the Revelation): "seven angels with the seven last plagues."

There was a sea of glass mixed with fire, which depicts the glory and majesty of God in heaven. He saw also the triumphant church — "those who had been victorious over the beast and his image and over the number of his name."

Accompanied by the harps they held in their hands, they sang a song of victory, which John calls "the song of Moses" and "the song of the Lamb." The song underscores what we learned about the 144,000 — both Old and New Testament believers make up the covenant community. This redemption song celebrates both the deliverance from Egyptian bondage and the believer's deliverance from the slavery of sin. Both redemptive acts were accomplished by the power of God and the blood of the Lamb.

After the song, the temple of God was opened. From it emerged the seven angels with their bowls of God's wrath. The picture unfolding is of God's final act of judgment in the history of the world against man's evil.

We don't like to think about or talk about the judgment of God. In his book *The Kingdom of God in America,* Reinhold Neibuhr observed:

> We want a God without wrath who took man without sin into a kingdom without justice through the ministrations of a Christ without a cross.

But judgment is real. Mark Twain once said, "It is not the parts of the Bible I don't understand that trouble me; it's the parts I do understand." The awesome judgment of God is a troubling reality.

John sees God's final judgment against sin in a vision of seven bowls of wrath that are poured out on the earth. He is careful to tell us that these are the "seven last plagues — last, because with them God's wrath is completed" (15:1). After they are poured out, the kingdom of God will come with power at the second coming of Christ. Evil will be removed. The unholy trinity will be destroyed forever. And there will be a new heaven and a new earth.

These seven plagues remind us of the plagues on Egypt (Exodus 7–11) and are similar in content to the seven trumpet judgments (Revelation 8–11). Only in John's vision are they all-inclusive in their impact. While the trumpet judgments affect a third of the earth, sea and humanity, the bowls are described as being poured out on the whole earth and on all the inhabitants of the earth, with the exception of those who belong to the Lord (see 6:10,11). It is important to remember that the righteous are always protected from these judgments (see 7:3). Note that the seventh trumpet leads into the seven last plagues.

John said that three woes are coming on the earth (see 8:13; 9:12; 11:14). The first woe, the fifth trumpet judgment, opens the Abyss so that demon locusts can roam the earth and torment humanity (9:1-12). The second woe, the sixth trumpet, prepares the way for Armageddon (9:13-21). The third woe (seventh trumpet) announces the kingdom of Christ and the seven last plagues (11:15-19).

NATURE AND HUMANITY
UNDER JUDGMENT

We now turn our attention to understand these seven last plagues as the angels pour out the bowls of wrath. The first four bowls affect nature and humanity (16:1-9):

✝ The first bowl is poured out on the land, and ulcerous sores afflict those with the mark of the Beast (v. 2).

✝ The second bowl is poured out on the sea. It turns to blood and every living thing in the sea dies (v. 3).

✝ The third bowl is poured out on the rivers and springs, and they become as blood (v. 4).

✝ The fourth bowl is poured out on the sun, and it is given power to scorch people with fire. Yet, the people of earth cursed God and refused to repent (vv. 8, 9).

The last three bowls are more spiritual in nature. Instead of nature and the natural world, they deal with spiritual influences. They usher in God's final act of judgment at Armageddon.

SPIRITUAL ENEMIES
UNDER JUDGMENT

✝ The fifth bowl is poured out on the throne of the Antichrist; his kingdom is plunged into darkness (16:10, 11).

✝ The sixth bowl is poured out on the Euphrates River. Its water dries up, enabling the kings of the East to cross as they are lured by the unholy trinity for "the battle on the great day of God Almighty" to the "place that in Hebrew is called Armageddon" (vv. 12-16).

✝ The seventh bowl is poured into the air. A loud voice from the throne proclaims, "It is finished!" God judges Babylon the Great and gives her the cup filled with the wine of the fury of His wrath (vv. 17-21).

This is one of the climaxes of the Revelation—the announcement "It is finished!" What a wonderful day it will be when evil is finished, human history as we know it is finished, and "the kingdom of the world has become the kingdom of our Lord and of his Christ, and he will reign for ever and ever" (11:15).

I am not being fatalistic about life here and now. I believe every person has a responsibility to make the world a better place for the glory of God and the good of all people. I believe we should vote our consciences, voice our views, and take every action possible politically, economically, socially and spiritually to improve our world.

But I'm realistic enough to know that there are limitations to our efforts because of the presence of evil in the world. Only when Jesus returns in glory can we ultimately say, "It is finished!" And the end of life as we know it will be the beginning of a new life in eternity.

Notice that John now pays great attention to the seventh bowl of wrath, God's judgment on Babylon. The next two chapters provide a graphic description on the rise and fall of Mystery Babylon the Great. Let's look at what he saw and learn about this subject, Babylon the Great.

THE RISE AND
FALL OF BABYLON

Historically, Babylon represents the world system in rebellion against God through civilizations and governments. It all began at the Tower of Babel, believed to be built by Nimrod and his followers when they rebelled against God (see Genesis 10; 11). *Babel*, the root of *Babylon*, means "confusion."

Later, the ancient Babylonian empire under king Nebuchadnezzar became the archenemy of Israel, eventually destroying Jerusalem and carrying the people into exile for 70 years. The early church referred to Rome as "Babylon" (see 1 Peter 5:13).

✝ Prophetically, the final expression of Babylon will be the Antichrist kingdom during the Tribulation.

✝ Specifically, Babylon is the religious side of Antichrist's empire that seeks to destroy the people of God.

✝ Spiritually, the symbol of Mystery Babylon the Great represents all political, commercial and religious systems in rebellion against God.

She is referred to many times in Revelation, and always as "Great." She is called "the great city that rules over the kings of the earth"(17:18). This is contrasted with the heavenly city, the New Jerusalem. We are reading about more than simply a literal, historical city of evil, such as Babylon or Rome or Sodom. The symbol of Mystery Babylon the

Great represents all systems of evil in the world that lure men away from God and seek to destroy the people of God.

Babylon is the spiritual mystery behind the horrendous slaughter of the righteous down through the ages. You can trace her evil works through Egypt, Babylon, Rome, Hitler's Nazi Germany, Mao's China, Stalin's Russia, Castro's Cuba, Saddam Hussein's Iraq, Pol Pot's Cambodia, and Ceausescu's Romania.

We see the influence of her spiritual corruption in Europe and America today. Make no mistake about it, Babylon the Great is on the earth today. Look closely at the details John gives.

She is called "the great prostitute" (17:1), which means she tempts us to commit spiritual adultery against the true and living God by following false gods.

She is contrasted with the wife of the Lamb, the bride, which represents Israel and the church (21:9). *Prostitution* here means idolatrous worship (see 2:14, 20). Note also that she seduces the world through abominations and magic spells (17:4; 18:23).

In the Old Testament other cities were described as harlots because of their idolatry: Nineveh (Nahum 3:4), Tyre (Isaiah 23:16, 17), Jerusalem (Ezekiel 16, 23), and Babylon (Jeremiah 51).

Ancient Babylon was built on the Euphrates River and boasted of a great aqueduct system of intricate water canals. Mystery Babylon sits on many waters: "Then the angel said to me, 'The waters you saw, where the prostitute sits, are peoples, multitudes, nations and languages' " (Revelation 17:15).

The many waters speak of her global influence. The kings of the earth commit adultery with spiritual Babylon. Nations and rulers are depicted as drunk on the wine of economic success and world power. Do we not see her influence today as we look at the nations and leaders of the world, intoxicated with power, prestige and pleasure?

The scarlet beast on which the prostitute rides is the Antichrist. The seven heads on the beast again speak of his universal wisdom; and the 10 horns, the strength of his political kingdom.

The gaudy prostitute's appearance is a paradox. On one hand she is beautifully arrayed in purple and scarlet, the colors of royalty. She glitters with gold, precious stones and pearls. Yet, she is detestable.

The golden cup in her hand is filled with many abominable things. Worse, she herself is intoxicated — drunk with the blood of the saints.

Her title, "Mystery Babylon the Great," carries its own significance. The word *mystery* means that which was hidden previously but is now revealed openly (see 1:20; 10:7).

She is called "the mother of prostitutes and of the abominations of the earth"(17:5). This means that she is the fountainhead of all anti-God forces in the world.

What are these abominations? An abomination is something evil and detestable in the eyes of God. Proverbs 6:16–19 tells us:

> *There are six things the Lord hates, seven that are detestable to him: haughty eyes, a lying tongue, hands that shed innocent blood, a heart that devises wicked schemes, feet that are quick to rush into evil, a false witness who pours out lies and a man who stirs up dissension among brothers.*

The list doesn't include all sins people commit but you can get the picture.

SORTING OUT
THE MEANING

We need to sort out the meaning of Mystery Babylon that the angel gave to John. This next passage in the Revelation is difficult to understand. When you read it the first time, you may be puzzled. You'll probably say, "Run that by me again."

Then the angel said to me: "Why are you astonished? I will explain to you the mystery of the woman and of the beast she rides, which has the seven heads and ten horns. The beast, which you saw, once was, now is not, and will come up out of the Abyss and go to his destruction. The inhabitants of the earth whose names have not been written in the book of life from the creation of the world will be astonished when they see the beast, because he once was, now is not, and yet will come.

"This calls for a mind with wisdom. The seven heads are seven hills on which the woman sits. They are also seven kings. Five have fallen, one is, the other has not yet come; but when he does come, he must remain for a little while. The beast who once was, and now is not, is an eighth king. He belongs to the seven and is going to his destruction.

"The ten horns you saw are ten kings who have not yet received a kingdom, but who for one hour will receive authority as kings along with the beast. They have one purpose and will give their power and authority to the beast" (17:7-13).

Let's look at this explanation section by section. First, the beast is the Antichrist.

Next, the seven heads are seven kings, or kingdoms, which are amalgamated with the Antichrist's kingdom. They represent historical kingdoms that have persecuted the people of God down through the ages. Some see in this description a specific parallel to the seven hills on which ancient Rome was built and the Roman emperors who persecuted the church. As such, they are a type of the coming Antichrist kingdom.

Symbolic language is used to describe the gradual demise of the Antichrist kingdom over a period of time. Five kings have already fallen, another falls, then the ending comes with complete destruction. Remember that the number *seven* means completion. These seven heads, then, are a part of the complete Antichrist empire, not separate kingdoms.

The description of the Antichrist as a being who "once was, now is not, and will come up out of the Abyss" (v. 8) probably is the same one John saw in the earlier vision arising out of the sea. There he sees him recover from a near-fatal wound (see 13:3). This seemingly miraculous recovery, either personally or politically, will cause the whole world to be astonished and to follow him.

The eighth king is the Antichrist. This means that he is the composite of all the worst of the evil rulers who have lived before him. The 10 kings, or kingdoms, John sees make up the Antichrist's confederacy. This alliance also consists of other nations which will give their authority and power to him.

Where is all of this heading? Toward God's overthrow of the Antichrist kingdom at Armageddon. John goes on to tell us:

> "They will make war against the Lamb, but the Lamb will overcome them because he is Lord of lords and King of kings – and with him will be his called, chosen and faithful followers."

> Then the angel said to me, "The waters you saw, where the prostitute sits, are peoples, multitudes, nations and languages. The beast and the ten horns you saw will hate the

prostitute. They will bring her to ruin and leave her naked; they will eat her flesh and burn her with fire. For God has put it into their hearts to accomplish his purpose by agreeing to give the beast their power to rule, until God's words are fulfilled. The woman you saw is the great city that rules over the kings of the earth" (17:14-18).

Here we see a preview of Armageddon when Jesus Christ returns at the end of the Great Tribulation. God is sovereign, even over the Antichrist. He will cause the Antichrist to turn on Babylon and destroy her in the same way He used Pharaoh to fulfill His purpose in the Exodus. Note the phrase "until God's words are fulfilled." This means that the will of God for us will be completed. Nothing can stop or hinder what God has planned for His people in eternity.

After this comes the heavenly announcement, "Fallen! Fallen is Babylon the Great!" (18:2). Kings, merchants and seamen who have prospered by their allegiance to Babylon greet this announcement with loud lament (18:9-20).

But she who deceived the nations, martyred the saints and conquered nations in her greed will meet a swift and complete destruction at Armageddon. It is interesting to note that the angel of the Revelation announces Mystery Babylon's demise in the same way that the Old Testament prophets Isaiah and Jeremiah announced the destruction of ancient Babylon (compare 18:21-24 with Isaiah 21:9 and Jeremiah 51:8).

WINNING
THE WAR

The key passage in this whole drama is Revelation 17:14: "They will make war against the Lamb, but the Lamb will overcome them because he is Lord of lords and King of kings — and with him will be his called, chosen and faithful followers." Obviously, this is a description of Armageddon. But spiritually we know that a war is being waged against the people of God now.

So this war against the Lamb is both current and future. Today, every believer faces the reality of spiritual warfare. Tomorrow, Armageddon will come. Three cardinal virtues of the overcoming church are given by John — called, chosen and faithful.

Called. Everyone is called by God to salvation. No one is left out. Jesus died for the sins of the whole world. Peter says, "The Lord is . . . patient with you, not wanting anyone to perish, but everyone to come to repentance" (2 Peter 3:9).

Every person who answers God's calling to salvation is also called to service. You will make an eternal contribution with your life only when you find your place of service for Christ. And that's what we all want out of life, isn't it? To make a contribution? To feel like the world is a little better off because you were here? Your calling in Christ will give you the greatest sense of significance you will ever know. It's amazing to think of the difference we can make if we will only fulfill the calling God places on our lives.

Former President Reagan often told the story of *Telemachus*, a fourth-century Christian, whose boldness for Christ made a difference in his generation. The Asian hermit lived in a remote village, tending his garden and spending much of his time in prayer.

One day he thought he heard the voice of God telling him to go to Rome so he obeyed, setting out on foot. Weeks later, he arrived in the city at the time of a great festival. The little monk followed the crowd surging down the streets into the Coliseum. He saw the gladiators stand before the emperor and heard them say, "We who are about to die salute you." Then he realized that these men were going to fight to the death for the entertainment of the crowd. He cried out, "In the name of Christ, stop!"

As the games began, he pushed his way through the crowd, climbed over the wall, and dropped to the floor of the arena. When the crowd saw the tiny figure rush to the gladiators and say, "In the name of Christ, stop!" they began to laugh.

Then they realized this wasn't a part of the show, and their laughter turned to anger. As Telemachus pled with the gladiators to stop, one of them plunged a sword into his body. The Christian martyr fell to the ground and his last words were, "In the name of Christ, stop!"

Then a strange thing happened. The gladiators stood looking at the tiny figure lying there. A hush fell over the Coliseum. Way up in the upper rows, a man stood and made his way to the exit. Others began to follow. In dead silence, everyone left the Coliseum.

The year was A.D. 391, and that was the last battle to the death between gladiators in the Roman Coliseum. Never again in the great stadium did men kill each other for the entertainment of the crowd. It was all because of one tiny voice that could hardly be heard above the tumult — one voice, one life that spoke the truth in God's name.

Chosen. Jesus put it this way: "You did not choose me, but I chose you and appointed you to go and bear fruit — fruit that will last. Then the Father will give you whatever you ask in my name" (John 15:16). That should keep every one of us from getting the bighead, thinking that we chose Christ. He chose us because He loves us. As chosen people we are called to pull away from the lure of Babylon with its immorality and idolatry. God says of Babylon, "Come out of her, my people, so that you will not share in her sins" (Revelation 18:4). This was the same message Jeremiah gave the people of God about ancient Babylon (see Jeremiah 50:8; 51:6-9). Isaiah issued the same call: "Come out from it and be pure, you who carry the vessels of the Lord" (Isaiah 52:11).

To be chosen means that we are special to God. As special people we live by a different code than does the world. I like the daily spiritual evaluation John Wesley and the members of his Holy Club would give themselves in their private devotions. I read it often because it helps me remember the joy and the responsibility of being chosen.

1. Am I consciously or unconsciously creating the impression that I am a better person than I really am? In other words, am I a hypocrite?

2. Am I honest in all my acts and words, or do I exaggerate?

3. Do I confidentially pass on what was told to me in confidence?

4. Can I be trusted?

5. Am I a slave to dress, friends, work or habit?

6. Am I constantly self-conscious, self-pitying, or self-justifying?

7. Did the Bible live in me today?

8. Do I give God time to speak to me every day?

9. Am I enjoying prayer?

10. When did I last speak to someone else of my faith?

11. Do I pray about the money I spend?

12. Do I get to bed on time and get up on time?

13. Do I disobey God in anything?

14. Do I insist on doing something about which my conscience is uneasy?

15. Am I defeated in any part of my life?

16. Am I jealous, impure, irritable, touchy, or distrustful?

17. How do I spend my spare time?

18. Am I proud?

19. Do I thank God I am unlike people, especially the Pharisees who despised the publican?

20. Is there anyone I fear, dislike, criticize or resent? If so, what am I doing about it?

21. Do I grumble and complain constantly?

22. Is Christ real to me?

So many people today don't feel special. They can identify with Charlie Brown. One day he was talking with Linus about the sense of inadequacy he feels all the time.

"You see, Linus," Charlie moaned, "it goes all the way back to the beginning. The moment I was born and set foot on the stage of life, they took one look at me and said, 'Not right for the part.' "

You cannot read the Bible seriously and not come face to face with the joyful reality that you are God's masterpiece! The psalmist pondered the majesty and glory of being human when he asked "What is man?" He came to understand that we are made a little lower than the angels, we are crowned with glory and honor, and we have been given dominion over the works of God's hands (Psalm 8).

Besides, in Christ the believer has a new self-image. This is why Paul stressed the concept of being "in Christ." In fact, he uses the term 172 times in his writings to describe the most intimate relationship possible with Christ.

✝ In Romans he says we are justified in Christ.

✝ In 1 Corinthians he says we are sanctified in Christ.

✝ In 2 Corinthians we are empowered in Christ.

✝ In Galatians we are liberated in Christ.

✝ In Ephesians we are gifted for service in Christ.

✝ In Philippians we are joyful in Christ.

✝ In Colossians we are complete in Christ.

✝ In 1 Thessalonians we are saved from wrath in Christ.

✝ In 2 Thessalonians we are glorified in Christ.

✝ In 1 Timothy we are given mercy in Christ.

✝ In 2 Timothy we are secure in Christ.

✝ In Titus we are redeemed in Christ.

✝ In Philemon we are recipients of every good thing in Christ.

Christ doesn't refurbish us, He doesn't renovate us, He doesn't reeducate us, He doesn't repair us, He doesn't reorient us. Christ re-creates us so that in Him the old things pass away and all things become new!

The Bible tells us that we are:

— sons of God (John 1:12)

— heirs of God and co-heirs with Christ (Romans 8:17)

— saints (1 Corinthians 1:2)

— God's masterpiece (Ephesians 2:10)

— a chosen generation (1 Peter 2:9)

— a kingdom of priests (Revelation 1:6)

—the apple of God's eye (Deuteronomy 32:10)

—the Lord's treasured possession (Malachi 3:17).

Above all, "we are his people, and the sheep of his pasture" (Psalm 100:3).

By the way, have you ever read Zephaniah 3:17? "The Lord . . . will take great delight in you, he will quiet you with his love, he will rejoice over you with singing." You are chosen for greatness in Christ!

Faithful. The word stands on its own. It means to be true, trustworthy and reliable. Andre Crouch sings, "You can depend on me, Jesus." That's faithfulness. Paul addressed believers in Ephesus as "the faithful in Christ Jesus" (Ephesians 1:1). Jesus said, "Be faithful, even to the point of death, and I will give you the crown of life" (Revelation 2:10).

The ancient city of Pergamum was so wicked that Jesus described it as the city "where Satan has his throne." Yet, a believer who lived there proved his faithfulness to Christ by sacrificing his life. That man's name was Antipas. Jesus praised him in the Revelation as "my faithful witness" (2:13). He is the only martyr mentioned by name in the Book of Revelation.

Tradition tells us that Antipas was taken to a place for public execution by the Romans in an effort to stop the spread and influence of Christianity in the city. As he was led along, the Roman guard escorting him pleaded:

"Antipas, this is senseless. There's no reason for you to die. Just renounce your faith in Jesus as Lord. You can believe in Him privately; just renounce Him publicly."

"I can't do that."

"But you must; if you don't you will surely die this day," said the guard. Antipas again refused to renounce his faith.

Exasperated, the guard said, "Antipas, don't you realize that the whole world is against you?"

This faithful servant of Christ didn't hesitate. He responded boldly, "Well, then, Antipas is against the whole world."

And he took his faith to the grave that lonely day in Pergamum. That's faithfulness!

A spiritual war is being fought today. A battle rages between good and evil, between the church and the world system, between the spirit of Christ and the spirit of antichrist. One day it will all come to an abrupt end at the final Battle of Armageddon.

On that day, the unholy trinity — Satan, the Antichrist, and the False Prophet — will make war against the Lamb. But the Lamb will overcome them because He is Lord of lords and King of kings!

Jesus Christ and His church will rule and reign triumphantly!

And those with Him are *called*, *chosen* and *faithful*!

Chapter

8

Let us, with a gladsome mind,
Praise the Lord, for He is kind:
For His mercies aye endure,
Ever faithful, ever sure.

—John Milton in "Psalm 136"

LET US REJOICE AND BE GLAD!

Let us rejoice and be glad and give him glory!
For the wedding of the Lamb has come, and his
bride has made herself ready (Revelation 1:19).

When Robert Ingersol, the noted agnostic, died, his funeral notice read: "There will be no singing at the funeral." There was nothing to sing about. There was no resource of faith in the crucible of life . . . no sound of praise in the face of death.

How different was my experience at the funeral of one of our parishioners who died of cancer in her mid-40s. In spite of her illness, she possessed a vibrant faith that she shared openly and freely with everyone she met. On the day of her funeral, her husband shared how inspired he had been by her faith.

He said, "Often, I would stand next to her in church, knowing she was in tremendous pain. Yet, as the congregation sang she would lift her voice and give glory to God." Then he added, "She had peace in the midst of her pain."

Singing scarcely exists in religions outside of Judaism and Christianity. In the Old Testament the Psalms, or songs of praise, occupy a central place in the 39 books. Over 500,000 Christian hymns have been composed during the church age.

God's people have always been characterized by the song of the Lord. Perhaps the most distinguishing mark of the people of God is our praise. C.S. Lewis makes the point that "praise is inner health made audible."

Praise is key to maintaining spiritual, mental and emotional health. It strengthens Christlike attitudes, beliefs, values, philosophy of life and lifestyle. Praise is adoration of God, encompassing gratitude, celebration, thanksgiving, worship and blessing.

Praise is expressed through singing, lifting hands, dancing, clapping hands, testifying, kneeling and music. The word *praise* appears 200 times in Scripture. While the Hebrew Old Testament uses some 50 different words for *praise*, the most frequent is *halal* (99 times) meaning "to boast, to laud, to make show, to celebrate." Add the suffix *jah* (pronounced *yah*, for the name of God, Yahweh) and we have the premier word for praise, *hallelujah*, meaning "praise the Lord."

The word *hallelujah* appears only four times in the New Testament — and all in Revelation 19. In fact, there are more references to praise in the Revelation than any other book in the Bible except the Psalms. This means that Revelation is the hymnal of the New Testament.

Take a minute and look at the series of songs and shouts of praise that God has woven through the Revelation:

† The song of the angels (5:11, 12)

✝ The song of the elders, saints and all created beings (4:8-11)

✝ The new song of the redeemed (5:9, 10)

✝ The song of the great multitude in heaven (7:9, 10)

✝ The heavenly praise announcing the defeat of the devil (10:10–12)

✝ The praise of the seventh trumpet declaring, "The kingdom of the world has become the kingdom of our Lord and of his Christ, and he will reign for ever and ever" (11:15)

✝ The special song of the 144,000 (14:1-5)

✝ The victorious church singing the song of Moses and the song of the Lamb (15:1-4).

The crescendo of praise reaches its climax in "Heaven's Hallelujah Chorus." This passage is worth reading:

After this I heard what sounded like the roar of a great multitude in heaven shouting: "Hallelujah! Salvation and glory and power belong to our God, for true and just are his judgments. He has condemned the great prostitute who corrupted the earth by her adulteries. He has avenged on her the blood of his servants." And again they shouted: "Hallelujah! The smoke from her goes up for ever and ever.

The twenty-four elders and the four living creatures fell down and worshiped God, who was seated on the throne. And they cried: "Amen, Hallelujah!"

Then a voice came from the throne saying: "Praise our God, all you his servants, you who fear him, both small and great!"

Then I heard what sounded like a great multitude, like the roar of rushing waters and like loud peals of thunder, shouting: "Hallelujah! For our Lord God Almighty reigns. Let us rejoice and be glad and give him glory! For the wedding of the Lamb has come, and his bride has made herself ready (19:1–7).

What a paradox—the book that unfolds the terrible future and the judgments of God is a book of praise. Let these words reverberate in your mind until they become a part of your very nature: "Let us rejoice and be glad!"

Sometimes we lose our sense of praise and complain about bad times. It's like a woman who had gone through a divorce and was dealing with so many problems the day she came to see me for counseling. For 10 minutes I just sat and listened as she went through a litany of everything that was wrong in her life. Then she stopped abruptly and said, "Listen to me. I sound just like a country and western song!"

Paul the apostle tells us, "Rejoice in the Lord always. I will say it again: Rejoice!" (Philippians 4:4). A tall order, to say the least. We can't help but ask, Why should we rejoice?

LET US REJOICE
GOOD TRIUMPHS OVER EVIL!

You have to believe that the goodness of God will ultimately triumph over evil if you're going to keep your joy. The first two hallelujahs affirm this great truth. They announce the defeat and destruction of Mystery Babylon the Great.

Throughout the Revelation we see great portraits of evil. We see the Dragon, the devil himself. We see the Antichrist and the False Prophet. We see the judgment of God as well as man's inhumanity to man. We see the seven last plagues. We see evil so deeply entrenched in the hearts of some that people refuse to repent of their sins, even in the face of judgment.

When we read all of this we have a tendency to become discouraged. But then the good news of Revelation shines through. The goodness of God will prevail. The church will be victorious. History will culminate in a new heaven and a new earth under the lordship of Jesus Christ. That's why heaven bursts forth in shouts of "Hallelujah!"

Not only will good win over evil in eternity, God's goodness will prevail in your life now, regardless of what you're facing. I find it helpful to reflect on the goodness of God in a world where bad things happen. It's true — life is hard and life is unfair. Bad things do happen to good people. But in the midst of it all, God is good.

David declared, "I am still confident of this: I will see the goodness of the Lord in the land of the living" (Psalm 27:13). Nahum assures us, "The Lord is good, a refuge in times of trouble. He cares for those who trust in him" (Nahum 1:7).

Jesus says, "If you, then, though you are evil, know how to give good gifts to your children, how much more will your Father in heaven give good gifts to those who ask him!" (Matthew 7:11).

The apostle Paul gives us one of the most profound truths for life: "And we know that in all things God works for the good of those who love him, who have been called according to his purpose" (Romans 8:28). This may be the most reassuring promise of God in the entire Bible. God is always working for your good in every situation you face.

This is not to suggest that God causes everything. He doesn't. God is not the source of trouble, hardship and suffering. But Paul says that "in all things" God works as a master sculptor to conform us to the image of Christ.

In the 15th century a genius was born into the world — Michelangelo. He was not only a master sculptor but also an artist, an architect, a painter and a scientist.

His number one love was sculpting. He gave us such masterpieces as *David, The Pieta, Moses* and *The Bacchus.*

He often described the art of sculpting as "the making of men." He considered the marble stone a prison which held captive living figures. "Freeing men from the prison of stone" is how he described his work.

That's exactly how God works in our lives. He chips away the excess stone until only the image of Christ remains. Goodness is our weapon in spiritual warfare. You can never win the war by fighting evil with evil. Paul put it this way: "Do not be overcome by evil, but overcome evil with good" (Romans 12:21). So let us rejoice and be glad — good will triumph over evil.

When bad times come our way, we can respond in a variety of ways:

1. *We can worry.* The Greek word for *worry* means "to be divided" or "inwardly distracted." The English word comes from an Anglo-Saxon root meaning "to choke or strangle." E. Stanley Jones said, "Worry is the sand in the machinery of life."

On a humorous note, worry is today's mouse eating tomorrow's cheese. Or, worry is like a rocking chair: it gives you something to do but gets you nowhere.

I like the beatitude that says, "Blessed is the man who is too busy to worry during the day, and too sleepy to worry at night."

2. *We can complain like ancient Israel in the wilderness.* They complained constantly against the Lord and the leadership of Moses. Even though God gave them one miracle after another, they forgot His goodness and doubted His promises.

Their constant complaining led them into such unbelief that what should have been a temporary passage through the desert became a 40-year excursion in the hot, dry wilderness of Judea.

3. *We can rebel.* Israel's complaint of the desert conditions eventually led them into rebellion against God. They built a golden calf and turned away from the Lord.

4. *We can feel sorry for ourselves.* All of us have been down the self-pity road, singing the old spiritual, "Nobody knows the trouble I've seen." Like Elijah the prophet we sit under a juniper tree and say, "Lord, I'm the only one You've got left."

If that is true, God is in serious trouble! But there is a better way: Let us rejoice and be glad! Why? The goodness of God will overcome all the problems we face and trials we endure. C.S. Lewis said, "God whispers to us in our pleasure, speaks in our conscience, but shouts in our pain."

No one is exempt from bad times. What you do when life hurts is the thing that really counts. E. Stanley Jones said, "Bitterness comes to all; it sours some, sweetens others. I shall use it to sweeten my spirit."

Our congregation, the Mount Paran Church of God, has an outreach ministry in Atlanta's inner city. Leon—homeless, destitute and on drugs—came to the mission one day and accepted Christ into his heart. His whole life began to turn around.

The pastor began teaching the people the importance of having a dream for their lives. They began to pray for each other's dreams to come to pass.

Leon's dream was to be a Marta bus driver. So, he completed the necessary training and went for the interview. A few days later he received a letter of rejection. He was very discouraged. But the pastor told him, "Don't give up. This is your dream. Let's pray and continue to trust the Lord to work this out."

Leon went back to his regular job. After a few days, he felt strangely impressed during lunch one day to call Marta, Atlanta's transit system. At first he resisted the urge, but the feeling was so strong that he finally gave in. From a pay phone he got the personnel department and introduced himself.

The lady at Marta said, "Thank God you called. The letter of rejection we sent you was a mistake. You have been accepted. Can you be here tomorrow to start your new job?" He couldn't believe it. In all things, God was working for his good.

Now that may seem incredibly insignificant to you, but not to Leon. He learned to rejoice because good triumphs over evil. He told the pastor that he looked forward to the day when he could give financial support to the ministry downtown. At first he would put only a few cents in the offering. He gradually increased the amount.

He now recalls how good it felt when he put his first $100 bill in the offering. He is able to give much more now because of the blessings of God in his life. His dream was not only for himself; his dream included helping others. And that's a dream God will bless.

LET US REJOICE FOR
GOD REIGNS OVER ALL!

What a fantastic declaration: "Hallelujah! For our Lord God Almighty reigns. Let us rejoice and be glad" (Revelation 19:6,7). The theme of Revelation, as in Daniel, is the *sovereignty* of God. That word simply means that God rules and reigns as the ultimate authority over all creation. Remember that the primary symbol of the book is the throne of God. It is mentioned 45 times, underscoring the fact that God is sovereign.

We worry and fret so much because we lose sight of the sovereignty of God. The classic example of a person who learned the hard way that God rules over all was the ancient Babylonian king, Nebuchadnezzar.

One day he walked out on the balcony of his palace. Gazing at the magnificence and grandeur of the city of Babylon with its majestic hanging gardens, he boasted, "Is not this the great Babylon I have built as the royal residence, by my mighty power and for the glory of my majesty?" (Daniel 4:30).

As the words came from his lips, he literally snapped. Immediately he was afflicted with a psychotic disorder called *zoanthropy*, and was reduced to acting like a brute beast of the field. His skin was toughened by the hot, arid climate of Iraq. His hair grew long, matted and coarse. His fingernails grew like talons!

Talk about falling off a pedestal!

But then Nebuchadnezzar made a comeback. Listen to his own testimony, published and distributed throughout the kingdom:

> *At the end of that time, I, Nebuchadnezzar, raised my eyes toward heaven, and my sanity was restored. Then I praised the Most High; I honored and glorified him who lives forever. His dominion is an eternal dominion; his kingdom endures from generation to generation. . . .*
>
> *At the same time that my sanity was restored, my honor and splendor were returned to me for the glory of my kingdom. My advisers and nobles sought me out, and I was restored to my throne and became even greater than before.*

Now I, Nebuchadnezzar, praise and exalt and glorify the King of heaven, because everything he does is right and all his ways are just. And those who walk in pride he is able to humble (Daniel 4:34, 36, 37).

When John tells us of the sovereignty of God, he calls Him "the Almighty." The Greek *pantokrator* literally means "the one who controls all things." It is used 10 times in the New Testament. Once Paul used this title when quoting from the Old Testament (2 Corinthians 6:18).

The other nine times occur in the Revelation, where it is the distinct title of God. When the Revelation was written, the world was under the domination of Rome; the church was seriously threatened by the powers of the state. Fear abounded. A note of uncertainty filled the air. Yet John calls God "the Almighty" — the One who controls all things.

So if you want to keep your joy in the midst of life's uncertainties, you must learn to declare: "Hallelujah! The Lord our God the Almighty reigns."

✝ When you see the troubling signs of the times fulfilled, don't get alarmed, say, "Hallelujah! The Lord our God the Almighty reigns."

✝ When false christs and false prophets appear, say, "Hallelujah! The Lord our God the Almighty reigns."

✝ When you hear of wars and rumors of wars, say, "Hallelujah! The Lord our God the Almighty reigns."

✝ When you receive bad news or face difficult circumstances, declare in faith, "Hallelujah! The Lord our God the Almighty reigns."

When President Abraham Lincoln was assassinated, most of this country went into mourning. There was confusion, despair and hopelessness. In New York City an anxious crowd gathered to express their grief over Lincoln's tragic death and their alarm about the future. Suddenly a man climbed the stairs of a building so he could look over the crowd. He shouted, "The Lord reigns over Washington!"

The people grew silent as the impact of his words brought them assurance that God was still in control. Slowly they began to disperse and go about their business.

You see, you can respond to the evil of this world, or the bad news you get in life, with negativism or with praise. A minister friend of mine was the guest speaker at a leadership retreat for our congregation. I sat spellbound as I listened to his testimony of healing from cancer. He had battled the disease for two years.

The most touching part was when he said that during that time he never became angry with God. Instead, every day he thanked the Lord for another day to live and sought to live it the best he could for the glory of God. What a difference in our attitude toward life when we really believe that God is sovereign and that He works all things together for our good.

That's what happened to George Frederick Handel when he wrote *The Messiah*. In 1741, Handel was depressed, in debt and without hope. He was 57 years old. One day a minor poet named Charles Jenners delivered to Handel a collection of Biblical excerpts titled *A Sacred Oratorio*. Somewhat nonchalantly Handel began reading its contents: "He was wounded for our transgressions and bruised for our iniquities . . . He was a man of sorrows, acquainted with grief."

Handel began to identify with the sufferings of the Messiah. The Spirit of the Lord touched his heart as he began to read words which lifted his eyes to behold the greatness of God: "Now the kingdom of this world has become the kingdom of our God and of His Christ, and He will reign forever and ever."

With divine inspiration, Handel began to compose a musical score to the lyrics. In seclusion for 24 days, he often went without food. At times, he said, he was so overwhelmed with joy that he would jump to his feet and shout, "Hallelujah!"

Later, when someone asked how he came to compose *The Messiah* in a mere 24 days, he said, "I saw heaven opened before me and God Almighty seated on His glorious throne." At an early performance in London, the King stood at the singing of the "Hallelujah Chorus" in honor of the true king, Jesus Christ. Since that time audiences have stood whenever it is sung.

This is exactly what we need to lift us out of the depths of depression—to see the glorious throne of the sovereign God and shout triumphantly, "Hallelujah! The Lord our God the Almighty reigns."

LET US REJOICE
THE FUTURE IS FANTASTIC!

The third reason we need to "rejoice and be glad" is that we are invited to the Marriage Supper of the Lamb. What's that? you may be asking. Well, both Israel and the church are described in the Bible as the wife of Jehovah and the bride of Christ respectively (see Jeremiah 2:2; Isaiah 54:5; Matthew 9:15; 2 Corinthians 11:2, 3).

At the end of Armageddon we read about the great supper of God (see Revelation 19:17). The feast we are focusing on is the wedding supper of the Lamb.

When I read this wedding analogy, I immediately think of the beauty of my wedding to Barbie and the vows we shared. As a pastor I've had the privilege of conducting countless weddings during my ministry. But the most fascinating wedding I've ever seen was in India.

The bridegroom was escorted to the home of the bride riding a beautiful white stallion. The groom wore an elegantly embroidered robe. The horse was covered with a beautiful silk blanket, saddle and headpiece made of costly materials. Precious stones and hundreds of mirror-like jewels reflected the light of the torches carried by the friends in the procession. Torches lit up the night; sounds of laughter and singing filled the air. It was a beautiful sight to behold.

But the greatest wedding of all will take place when Jesus translates His people into heaven and we are one with Him in eternity. What does the bride analogy teach us about the Christian life? I'm not so sure everybody is as positive as they need to be about marriage today. I ran across these "new" definitions of marriage:

- Marriage is a three-ring circus: first you have the engagement ring, then the wedding ring and, finally, the "suffe-*ring*."

- Marriage is an adventure. It's like going off to war.

- Here's my favorite: Marriage is like a midnight phone call—you get a ring and then you wake up!

But the marriage relationship is a great example of our relationship with the Lord.

First of all, marriage is a relationship of love. It's all about falling in love and staying in love. So is the Christian life. The greatest of all commandments is, "Love the Lord your God." The entire gospel of Christ is summed up in the golden text of the Bible: "For God so loved the world that he gave his only begotten son . . ." (John 3:16). A relationship with God is more than ritualism, ceremonies, sacraments and good works.

Instead, it is a relationship of loving and being loved. What a tragedy to lose our sense of love for God. We lose the joy of this relationship when we get caught up in the trappings of religious works. That's what happened to the church at Ephesus. Jesus said to them,

> "I know your deeds, your hard work and your perseverance. I know that you cannot tolerate wicked men, that you have tested those who claim to be apostles but are not, and have found them false. You have persevered and have endured hardships for my name, and have not grown weary." All of that may have had its place, but they forgot the main thing. "Yet," He continued, " I hold this against you: You have forsaken your first love" (Revelation 2:2-4).

What is the first love? It is the passionate, all-consuming force of love that draws us into the covenant of marriage. Don't lose your first love for Christ. As Jude says, "Keep yourselves in God's love"(v. 21).

Marriage is also a relationship of loyalty. Without faithfulness to the wedding vows, marriage is an utter impossibility. Sometimes the vows don't come out exactly like we planned them.

I'll never forget a particular wedding I performed. The groom was very nervous, but he was doing fine until we got to the ring ceremony. As he placed the ring on the bride's finger, he was to repeat after me, "And all my worldly goods to share." He said, "and all my worldly *girls* to share."

But in marriage you have to forsake the girls to have *the girl.* Marriage is a covenant, not a contract. Covenant love is *unconditional love.* It is *selfless love,* even as Christ Jesus

204

made Himself of no reputation. It is *serving love*, even as He wrapped a towel around His waist and washed the feet of His disciples at the Last Supper. It is *sacrificial love*, even as He stretched Himself out on the cross and died for the sins of the world. "For God so loved the world that He gave."

That's the kind of love that makes marriage meaningful. Such indestructible, undying love is the eternal bond between a husband and wife. It holds them together through thick and thin, through ups and downs, and through mountain peaks and valleys. In the same way, believers are loyal to Jesus Christ as He is loyal to us.

Marriage is also an intimate relationship. The marriage relationship is so close that God says "two become one flesh." Jesus challenged the Laodiceans, "Behold, I stand at the door and knock" (Revelation 3:20, *KJV*). They had lost the intimacy of His presence in their church. Jesus was on the outside longing to be with them, but they had pushed Him out.

Paul the apostle expressed his desire for spiritual intimacy when he revealed his single motive in life, "I want to know Christ" (Philippians 3:10). Christ doesn't call us into the trappings of religion . . . He calls us into a loving relationship.

Marriage is a joyful relationship. That's why the wedding is described as a great feast of rejoicing. Marriage is a gift from God to bring unspeakable joy and companionship for life.

Jesus wants us to be joyful: "I have told you this so that my joy may be in you and that your joy may be complete" (John 15:11). Jesus was joyful and He desires to pour His joy into our hearts as we follow Him wholeheartedly.

A young daughter came to her father one day and said, "Dad, Tom has asked me to marry him."

"That's great, sweetheart," her father replied.

"But," she said, "I don't know what to do."

Her father replied, "What do you mean you don't know what to do? This is what you've always wanted."

"I know, Daddy, but I can't stand the thought of leaving Mother."

"Well, don't let that stop you—take your mother with you!"

Finally, marriage is a relationship that takes perseverance. Every couple who stays together for life learns to stick together when times get tough. If the Book of Revelation has given us any principle, it has taught us that we must persevere in our faith regardless of what comes our way.

This is what Jesus meant when He said, "He who stands firm to the end will be saved" (Matthew 24:13). It's not how you start the race of faith that counts, it is how you finish. So, finish well. Just as marriage is a lifelong commitment—till death us do part—so is the Christian life.

Jesus Christ has committed Himself to see you through to the end. Are you just as committed to Him? Have you responded to the invitation sent by the Holy Spirit?

Remember the words, "Blessed are those who are invited to the wedding supper of the Lamb." Everyone is invited but not all respond. In the words of Jesus, "Many are called, but few are chosen"(Matthew 22:14, *KJV*). Those who are blessed are those who have responded to the invitation to trust Christ as their Savior and Lord.

The kingdom of heaven is like a wedding feast, Jesus said:

The kingdom of heaven is like a king who prepared a wedding banquet for his son. He sent his servants to those who had been invited to the banquet to tell them to come, but they refused to come.

Then he sent some more servants and said, "Tell those who have been invited that I have prepared my dinner: My oxen and fattened cattle have been butchered, and everything is ready. Come to the wedding banquet."

But they paid no attention and went off — one to his field, another to his business. . . .

Then he said to his servants, "The wedding banquet is ready, but those I invited did not deserve to come. Go to the street corners and invite to the banquet anyone you find." So the servants went out into the streets and gathered all the people they could find, both good and bad, and the wedding hall was filled with guests. . . .

For many are invited, but few are chosen (Matthew 22:2-5, 8-10, 14).

Frederick the Great of Prussia invited Voltaire, the noted French atheist, to a banquet. During the toast Voltaire boasted, "I will trade my place in heaven for one Prussian mark."

After a silence a fellow guest said to Voltaire, "Sir, in Prussia we have a law that says before we can sell anything, we have to have proof of ownership. Can you prove that you have a seat in heaven?"[1]

Can *you*?

Chapter
9

We don't like to think that our carefully made plans, our long-range schemes may be interrupted by the trumpet of God. Too many people would rather say, "Oh well, the end of the world hasn't come yet, so why think about it—it's probably a thousand years away."

– Billy Graham
quoted in George Sweeting's *Who Said That?*)

DATELINE: ARMAGEDDON

Then they gathered the kings together to a place that in Hebrew is called Armageddon (Revelation 16:16).

*A*rmageddon! The word alone strikes a note of fear in the human heart. The very mention of Armageddon conjures images of nuclear holocaust, World War III, and the end of the world.

A *U. S. News & World Report* poll found that nearly 60 percent of Americans think the world will end some time in the future. Almost a third of those think it will end within a few decades. Nearly half believe a literal antichrist will arise, and 44 percent believe the Battle of Armageddon will occur.[1]

The end of the world no longer seems a far-fetched idea. Charles B. Strozier, psychoanalyst and history professor at the City University of New York, said, "We no longer need poets to tell us it could all end with a bang, or a whimper, or in the agony of AIDS. With the looming possibility of nuclear or environmental destruction, it now takes an active imagination *not* to think about human endings."

Many people today believe that the turn of the century will usher in the millennial kingdom of Christ. Ted Daniels, editor of *Millennial Prophecy Report*, notes that there is a broad expectation that "when the world's odometer ticks over to three zeros, it will have cosmic significance."[2]

Why has this ancient Hebrew word *Armageddon* taken on such global significance in recent years? For our answer we turn to the Bible, God's Word, where we find the origin of Armageddon.

ARMAGEDDON
AN HISTORICAL SITE

The word *Armageddon* appears only in the Book of Revelation, although its root word *Meggido* appears often in the Old Testament. Armageddon simply means the mount or hill (*har*) of Meggido.

Meggido was a Canaanite stronghold in the Jezreel plain in northern Israel and was captured by the Israelites during the campaigns of Joshua (Joshua 12:21; Judges 5:19). The valley begins at Meggido and stretches 200 miles south to the Gulf of Aquaba. It has been the site of many historic battles.

Here, Barak and Deborah conquered Sisera (Judges 5:19, 20), and King Ahaziah died by the arrows of Jehu (2 Kings 9:27). In this valley, the godly king Josiah died in battle with Pharaoh Necho (2 Kings 23:29, 30). Meggido was the location of Solomon's famed stables which held 450 chariot horses. The site has been extensively excavated. Napoleon called it one of the most natural battlefields in the world.

The prophet Joel called Megiddo the Valley of Jehoshaphat, which means "the Lord judges," and the Valley of Decision (Joel 3:2, 14). God declares that one day "I will gather all nations and bring them down to the Valley of Jehoshaphat. There I will enter into judgment against them concerning my inheritance, my people Israel" (Joel 3:2).

ARMAGEDDON
THE LAST WAR

It would be wonderful to think that we could achieve world peace through political diplomacy, economic justice, or the signing of peace treaties. But the Bible tells us clearly that this is not the case.

The prophet Daniel was clear that "war will continue until the end and desolations have been decreed" (Daniel 9:26). Concerning the last days Jesus said, "You will hear of wars and rumors of wars. . . . Nation will rise against nation, and kingdom against kingdom" (Matthew 24:6, 7).

The next time world leaders sit down at the table of global politics to negotiate a peace treaty, remember the prophecy of Paul: "While people are saying, 'Peace and safety,' destruction will come on them suddenly . . . and they will not escape" (1 Thessalonians 5:3).

The Old Testament provides a prophetic preview of the devastation that will be brought on by this terrible war in such passages as Ezekiel 38, 39; Zechariah 14; and Joel 3. When we come to the Book of Revelation we see a series of passages on the Battle of Armageddon. Let's take a closer look at what will happen on that awesome day.

We get our first glance at Armageddon in 14:19, 20:

> The angel swung his sickle on the earth, gathered its grapes and threw them into the great winepress of God's wrath. They were trampled in the winepress outside the city, and blood flowed out of the press, rising as high as the horses' bridles for a distance of 1,600 stadia.

So terrible will that day be that the Bible says the blood will flow as high as the horses' bridles for 200 miles. This same imagery is given in Isaiah 63:1-6. The awesome picture the prohet gives here is that of "a head-on battle, a great defeat of the enemy and a sea of spilled blood."[1]

The Revelator says the battle will take place "outside the city" — referring to the city of Jerusalem, both literally and spiritually. The Revelation only mentions two cities — the city of God, the new Jerusalem which represents the people of God; and the city of Babylon, which represents the present world system of evil.

Next, we read of Armageddon: "Then they gathered the kings together to the place that in Hebrew is called Armageddon" (Revelation 16:16). This describes the sixth bowl of wrath. The Euphrates River dries up, allowing the kings of the East to march across it toward Armageddon where God will war against them.

There is a striking parallel between the sixth bowl and the sixth trumpet, which also describes the drying up of the Euphrates. I point this out to underscore the repetitive nature of John's apocalyptic visions.

The sixth trumpet sounds and the angel is told:

> Release the four angels who are bound at the great river Euphrates. And the four angels who had been kept ready for this very hour and day and month and year were released to kill

*a third of mankind. The number of the mounted troops was two
hundred million. I heard their number* (9:14).

When the Revelation was written in the first century, it
was inconceivable to imagine an army from the East num-
bering 200 million. But today, with the armies of Red China
and other eastern nations, such a massive army assembled
at Armageddon is not beyond question.

What is the significance of the Euphrates River? The
Euphrates is the locale of the cradle of civilization, dating
back to the early Mesopotamian culture. Later, ancient
Babylon was built along the Euphrates.

After the Euphrates dries up, John sees evil spirits like
frogs come out of the mouth of the Dragon, the Beast and
the False Prophet. He says, "They are spirits of demons
performing miraculous signs, and they go out to the kings
of the whole world, to gather them for the battle on the
great day of God Almighty" (16:14).

As the satanic trinity, through demonic powers, persuade
nations, the kings of the East are lured into battle by the
these demon spirits which are compared to frogs.

The fact that they come out of the mouths of the Dragon
(Satan), the Beast (the Antichrist), and the False Prophet
tell us that these kings, or world leaders, fall under the hyp-
notizing power of the deceptive political rhetoric of the Antichrist propaganda.

Frogs were considered unclean by the Jews (see Leviticus
11:19, 41). This probably dates back to the plague of the
frogs on Egypt. That country considered the frog a symbol
of the goddess Heqt, who represented resurrection and fertility to them. The Persians thought the frog was a double
for Ahriman, god of evil and agent of plagues.[3]

ARMAGEDDON
A SPIRITUAL REALITY

Whatever you believe about the geographical location of Armageddon or the arrangement of nations that will be involved, one thing is certain: Armageddon is an apocalyptic figure that represents the final struggle between good and evil. It is more than a human war fought with human weapons of war.

In 16:16, we read that there are "spirits of demons" that draw the kings of the East into this battle—which means that this war is spiritually motivated. Armageddon is more than a geographic site. The word itself describes the final eschatological confrontation where God meets Satan in a final conflict and the forces of evil are defeated forever. The scholar, Mounce, makes the following observation:

> Har-Magedon is symbolic of the final overthrow of all the
> forces of evil by the might and power of God. The great
> conflict between God and Satan, Christ and Antichrist, good
> and evil, which lies behind the perplexing course of history
> will in the end issue in a final struggle in which God will
> emerge victorious and take with him all who placed their
> faith in him. This is Har-Magedon.[4]

Nevertheless, Armageddon refers equally to an actual date in future history and to real armies who will meet the judgment of God. At Armageddon, Jesus Christ will return to earth in the fulness of His power and glory to destroy the Antichrist kingdom and to establish the eternal kingdom of God. Paul declares of this day:

> This will happen when the Lord Jesus is revealed from heaven
> in blazing fire with his powerful angels. . . . Those who . . . do
> not obey the gospel of our Lord Jesus . . . will be punished with
> everlasting destruction and shut out from the presence of the

Lord and from the majesty of his power on the day he comes to
be glorified in his holy people and to be marveled at among all
those who have believed (2 Thessalonians 1:7-10).

To the Corinthians he wrote: "Then the end will come, when [Jesus] hands over the kingdom to God the Father after he has destroyed all dominion, authority and power. For he must reign until he has put all his enemies under his feet. The last enemy to be destroyed is death" (1 Corinthians 15:24-26). This is the triumphant side of Armageddon.

The second coming, or second advent, of Jesus is to be distinguished from the rapture of the church which will have already taken place at the beginning of the seven-year Great Tribulation period. While Jesus told us in no uncertain terms that no one knows the day or hour of His return, He did give us a prophetic profile of the last days (Matthew 24:1-14). The end of the world is, in reality, only the beginning of the new world order that will appear when Christ returns.

Three important Greek words in the New Testament describe the majesty of His coming. His coming will be a *parousia*. This means a personal appearing. The word was used to describe the appearance of a king in his royal procession when he paid a personal visit to a province in His kingdom.

Paul says, "The Lord Himself shall descend from heaven with a shout" (1 Thessalonians 4:16). Not an angel or a heavenly messenger or a prophet—but the Lord himself!

His coming will be an *epiphanea*. This means a sudden, triumphant and glorious appearing. Literally, the word describes a sudden burst of dazzling brilliance as the lightning illuminates the sky.

The Lord Jesus will come with the clouds of heaven and with the host of angels. He will come with glory:

✝ It will be the glory that filled the universe in the dawn of creation when God said,"Let there be light" (Genesis 1:3).

✝ It will be the glory that filled the temple of Solomon when it was dedicated (2 Chronicles 7:1).

✝ It will be the glory Isaiah saw in a vision of God (Isaiah 6:1-3).

✝ It will be the glory of the transfiguration experience as Moses and Elijah appeared with Jesus on the mountain (Matthew 17:2-6).

✝ It will be the glory that John saw in Jesus when he said, "His face was like the sun shining in all its brilliance" (1:16).

There will be nothing secretive about His return. The Bible says, "Every eye will see Him" (1:7). What a day that will be!

Finally, His coming will be an *apokolupsis,* which is the word translated "revelation." When Jesus returns, His deity will not be veiled by the garment of flesh as it was in His incarnation. We will see Him in the fulness of glory and power.

He will not return as the Christ of Bethlehem, or the Christ of the parables or the miracles, or the Christ of the cross; but as the Christ of the Advent who holds the keys of death and hell. The Revelator proclaims:

> *I saw heaven standing open and there before me was a white horse, whose rider is called Faithful and True. With justice he judges and makes war. His eyes are like blazing fire, and on his head are many crowns. He has a name written on him that no one knows but he himself. He is dressed in a robe dipped in blood, and his name is the Word of God. The armies of heaven were following him, riding on white horses and dressed in fine*

linen, white and clean. Out of his mouth comes a sharp sword with which to strike down the nations. "He will rule them with an iron scepter." He treads the winepress of the fury of the wrath of God Almighty. On his robe and on his thigh he has this name written: King of kings and Lord of lords (19:11-16).

This descriptive vision of Jesus is as awe-inspiring as the vision in chapter 1. John sees "heaven standing open." In 4:1, he saw heaven's door standing open. In 11:19, he saw the temple of heaven standing open.

Now, as the drama of history is coming to a climax, John sees all of heaven standing open so each one of us can see the purposes and plans of God coming into fulfillment. This whole scene unveils the triumphant glory of Jesus when He returns at Armageddon.

There before me was a white horse whose rider is called Faithful and True. The white horse symbolizes conquest and victory. This is not the white horse rider of the seven seals which describes the Antichrist (6:1). The Rider in chapter 19 is faithful and true. He keeps His word of promise and stands in stark contrast to the Antichrist who is full of deception and hypocrisy.

With justice He judges and makes war. Isaiah says that Messiah will rule the world with justice and righteousness (Isaiah 11:3). The war Christ wages is really the final skirmish in the war He fought at Calvary. Once and for all He defeated the powers of evil (see Colossians 2:13-15), and Armageddon is a mop-up operation for Him!

His eyes are like blazing fire, and on his head are many crowns. We have already seen His eyes of fire as He searches our hearts and minds (1:14; 2:18). On his head are not just seven crowns (12:3) or ten crowns (13:1), but many royal crowns signifying that he has all authority in heaven and on earth. The word for crown is *diadem*, as opposed to the word used for the victor's crown or wreath of victory.

He also has a name that no one knows but He himself. In addition to the names ascribed to Him in this vision— Faithful and True, the Word of God, and King of kings and Lord of lords—He has an unknown name. In ancient times, knowledge of the name of a god was associated with the power of that god. To know the name was to experience the power and presence of the god. The point made here is that no one can ever completely grasp the full power and person of Jesus.

No wonder the apostle Paul said: "I want to know Christ" (Philippians 3:10). He meant that knowing Jesus was an enriching, ever-expanding experience.

The *Amplified Bible* says: "That I may know Him—that I may progressively become more deeply and intimately acquainted with Him, perceiving and recognizing the wonders of His person more strongly and more clearly." We can know Him from *A* to *Z*, as:

A-lpha and Omega

B-eginning and the End

C-hief Cornerstone

D-aystar on high

E-mmanuel

F-aithful and true Witness

G-reat High Priest

H-oly One of Israel

I-mage of the invisible God

K-ing of kings

L-amb of God

M-ighty God

N-ew Covenant

O-vercomer

P-rince of peace

Q-uickener of the dead

R-ock of ages

S-avior of the world

T-ruth

U-ndeniable evidence

V-ictor over death, hell and the grave

W-ord of God

X-yster (a surgical cutting tool) of conviction

Y-ielded servant

Z-enith of truth.

But when we have finished with all the appropriate names for Him, we must then say: "He has a name that no man knows for He is wonderful beyond description!"

He is called the Word of God. The Jewish mind thought a word was more than the articulation of an idea, or even the mere making of sound. Words meant action. The creation account repeats the phrase, "And God said. . . ," (Genesis 1:4).

When Moses received the Law at Sinai, the writer records, "And God spoke all these words" (Exodus 20:1).

Jeremiah said that the word of God is like a hammer that breaks a rock into pieces and is like a consuming fire (Jeremiah 23:29).

Finally, the writer to the Hebrews tells us in no uncertain terms: "For the word of God is living and active. Sharper than any double-edged sword, it penetrates even to dividing soul and spirit, joints and marrow; it judges the thoughts and attitudes of the heart" (Hebrews 4:12).

John Paterson, in *The Book That Is Alive,* says: "The spoken word in Hebrew was fearfully alive. It was not merely a vocable or sound dropped heedlessly from unthinking lips. It was a unit of energy charged with power."[5]

Here we see the judgmental word of God in action. Moses fearlessly declared the coming plagues on Egypt, and his word became reality. In a greater way, the eternal word of God will be fulfilled concerning the final judgment. It is an unalterable reality.

Over and over we read the phrase in the Bible, "And it came to pass," reminding us of the fact that *not one word has failed of His good promise* (see 1 Kings 8:56).

Note that Jesus doesn't merely speak the word of God, He is the Word of God! This means that every messianic promise of the Old Testament was fulfilled in Him. Every human hope is met in Him. He is God's word of promise incarnate.

Now we see why the apostle John described the first coming of Jesus into the world by saying:

> *In the beginning was the Word, and the Word was with God, and the Word was God. He was with God in the beginning. Through him all things were made; without him nothing was made that has been made. In him was life, and that life was the light of men . . . The Word became flesh and made his dwelling among us. We have seen his glory, the glory of the One and Only, who came from the Father, full of grace and truth* (John 1:1-4, 14).

He is dressed in a robe dipped in blood. Three uses of blood appear in the Revelation. First, the sacrificial blood of Jesus shed at Calvary which has redeemed us from our sins is the source of our praise (5:9, 10).

Second, the blood of the martyrs which God has promised to avenge is prominent (6:10; 17:6).

Third, the blood which flows in the valley at Armageddon as He "treads the winepress of the fury of the wrath of God Almighty" (19:15b). This last reference is probably most consistent with the vision of Armageddon and correlates with Isaiah's vision of the final judgment (see Isaiah 63:1-6).

Yet, we do no harm to the passage when we see the beauty of all three truths. When Jesus returns, He will come in the power of His redemption to vindicate the cause of the afflicted and to bring Satan and his demonic helpers to their decisive end.

The armies which are in heaven follow Him. This triumphant army consists of both the angelic host and the raptured saints who have already celebrated the wedding supper of the Lamb in heaven and have received their rewards (Matthew 24:30-31).

The clothing of this army is white linen, and the fact that they follow the Rider is descriptive language used of believers throughout the Revelation (see 7:13; 14:17; 19:8).

Out of His mouth comes a sharp sword. This sword is the omnipotent power of His Word that we have already seen in John's first vision of Christ (1:16). Paul the apostle speaks of "the sword of the Spirit, which is the word of God" (Ephesians 6:17).

What is the purpose of this sword? "With it he will strike down the nations. He will rule them with an iron scepter."

What an astounding picture of complete judgment. The psalmist spoke prophetically of the Messiah king: "You will rule them with an iron scepter; you will dash them to pieces like pottery" (Psalm 2:9). Actually, the rod referenced here is the rod of a shepherd. Jesus will shepherd the nations in the millennial kingdom with the rod of perfect justice, true righteousness and everlasting peace (2:27).

On his robe and on his thigh he has the name written: King of kings and Lord of lords. His name is fully displayed for all to see. He comes as the absolute Lord and King, in the fulness of his power and authority.

When Queen Elizabeth was crowned by the Archbishop of Canterbury, he placed the crown on her head with the sure pronouncement, "I give thee, O Sovereign Lady, this crown to wear until He who reserves the right to wear it shall return."

How different the second coming of Christ will be from His first coming into the world. It's worth sitting up and taking notice of this difference!

- ✝ When He came the first time he was meek and lowly of heart, but He will return as Judge of all the earth.

- ✝ When He came the first time He was born in a manger, but when He returns He will be clothed with glory.

- ✝ When He came the first time He was given a reed for a scepter, but when He returns He will rule the nations with a rod of iron.

- ✝ When He came the first time He wore a crown of thorns, but when He returns He will be crowned with many crowns.

- ✝ When He came the first time He was despised, rejected, mocked, crucified; but when He returns every knee will bow to Him and every tongue will confess that Jesus Christ is Lord to the glory of God the Father.

THE GREAT
SUPPER OF GOD

The imagery of the great supper of God reflects back to Ezekiel 38 and 39, and the prophecy concerning Gog and Magog:

> *And I saw an angel standing in the sun, who cried in a loud voice to all the birds flying in midair, "Come, gather together for the great supper of God, so that you may eat the flesh of kings, generals, and mighty men, of horses and their riders, and the flesh of all people, free and slave, small and great."*
>
> *Then I saw the beast and the kings of the earth and their armies gathered together to make war against the rider on the horse and his army. But the beast was captured, and with him the false prophet who had performed the miraculous signs on his behalf. With these signs he had deluded those who had received the mark of the beast and worshiped his image. The two of them were thrown alive into the fiery lake of burning sulfur. The rest of them were killed with the sword that came out of the mouth of the rider on the horse, and all the birds gorged themselves on their flesh* (Revelation 19:17-21).

Look at Ezekiel's vision of Gog and Magog, the enemies of Israel:

> *"Son of man, prophesy against God and say: This is what the Sovereign Lord says: 'I am against you, O Gog, chief prince of Meshech and Tubal. I will turn you around and drag you along. I will bring you from the far north and send you against the mountains of Israel. Then I will strike your bow from your left hand and make your arrows drop from your right hand. On the mountains of Israel you will fall, you and all your troops and the nations with you. I will give you as food to all kinds of carrion birds and to the wild animals. You will fall in the open field, for I have spoken, declares the Sovereign Lord. I will*

send fire on Magog and on those who live in safety in the coastlands, and they will know that I am the Lord.'

"Son of man, this is what the Sovereign Lord says: Call out to every kind of bird and all the wild animals: 'Assemble and come together from all around to the sacrifice I am preparing for you, the great sacrifice on the mountains of Israel. There you will eat flesh and drink blood' " (Ezekiel 39:1-6, 17).

The imagery in John's vision is clearly related to Ezekiel's vision. While many scholars debate the details of Ezekiel's vision, and in particular, the identity of Gog and Magog, the overarching purpose of the vision is clear. God Almighty has set a day on which He will judge the world in triumph and truth through the One He has appointed judge of all men: Jesus Christ the Righteous.

THE GOD OF
BATTLES

Now for the bottom line: Any way you look at it, the Revelation is a book of victory. Its transcendent visions set forth the victory of God as He completes His purpose for Creation in a new heaven and a new earth.

The ultimate outcome of the Revelation demonstrates the victory of Jesus Christ in both His redemptive work and work of judgment when He returns. Clearly, they proclaim the victory of the church which, by faith, overcomes the world.

As the drama draws to a close we recount the defeat of those who bear the mark of the beast (15:1), the rise and fall of Babylon the Great (17:1), and now the defeat of the Antichrist and the False Prophet who are swiftly thrown into the lake of fire. The only figure left to be defeated is the Devil himself, and we will see his demise in the next chapter.

Wonderful! Magnificent! you say. But what principles can we gleam from this preview of Armageddon for our own lives here and now? The one principle of faith that emerges is the fact that God is the God of battles. Just as He will prevail in the last of all battles, He will fight for you in your own battles — battles against sin, self, stressful situations, sickness, and Satan himself.

This was the message of Moses to Israel at the Red Sea: "The Lord will fight for you; you need only to be still" (Exodus 14:14).

When David, the shepherd who became king, faced the Philistine champion, Goliath, he told him:

> "You come against me with sword and spear and javelin, but I come against you in the name of the Lord Almighty, the God of the armies of Israel, whom you have defied. This day the Lord will hand you over to me . . . and the whole world will know that there is a God in Israel" (1 Samuel 17:45, 46).

King Jehoshaphat sought the Lord for deliverance from allied forces that were in route to besiege Jerusalem. Then came the prophecy: "The battle is not yours, but God's."

After God fought their battle for them, "The fear of God came upon all the kingdoms of the countries when they heard how the Lord had fought against the enemies of Israel" (see 2 Chronicles 20:15, 29).

When Sennacherib of Assyria invaded Judah, King Hezekiah encouraged the nation with the announcement, "'With him is only the arm of flesh, but with us is the Lord our God to help us and to fight our battles.' And the people gained confidence from what Hezekiah the king of Judah said" (2 Chronicles 32:8). Scripture goes on to assure us:

✝ "Through you we push back our enemies; through your name we trample our foes" (Psalm 44:5).

✝ "In all these things we are more than conquerors through him who loved us" (Romans 8:37).

✝ "Everyone born of God overcomes the world. This is the victory that has overcome the world, even our faith" (1 John 5:4).

When you read the prophecy concerning Armageddon and realize that the God of battles will fight for you, you can't help but be filled with a spirit of triumphant faith that says with the apostle Paul: "If God be for us, who can be against us?" (Romans 8:31). This the real message of the Revelation!

During World War II, the Nazi army threatened to destroy England. In that crictical time in history, Winston Churchill motivated the troops and people of Britain with these words:

> I have nothing to offer but blood, toil, tears and sweat. Victory at all costs, victory in spite of all terror, victory however long and hard the road may be; for without victory there is no survival. . . .
>
> We shall not flag or fail. We shall go on to the end. We shall fight in France, we shall fight in the seas and oceans, we shall fight with growing confidence and growing strength in the air; we shall defend our island whatever the cost may be.
>
> We shall fight on the beaches, we shall fight on the landing grounds, we shall fight in the fields and in the streets, we shall fight in the hills; we shall never surrender.

We know that in the grand scheme of history, Christ and His cause will ultimately prevail and be victorious!

Chapter

10

Even the wilderness will rejoice in those days. The deserts will become as green as the mountains . . . as lovely as . . . Sharon. There the Lord will display . . . the splendor of our God. . . . He will open the eyes of the blind and unstop the ears of the deaf. The lame will leap like a deer, and those who cannot speak will shout and sing! . . . Sorrow and mourning will disappear, and they will be overcome with joy and gladness.

—Isaiah 35:1a, 2b, 5, 6, 10b, *NLT*

THEY REIGNED A THOUSAND YEARS WITH CHRIST

*I saw thrones on which were seated those who had been given author-
ity to judge. And I saw the souls of those who had been beheaded
because of their testimony for Jesus and because of the word of God.
Then had not worshiped the beast or his image and had not received
his mark on their foreheads or their hands. They came to life and
reigned with Christ a thousand years. (The rest of the dead did not
come to life until the thousand years were ended.) This is the first
resurrection. Blessed and holy are those who have part in the first
resurrection. The second death has no power over them, but they will
be priests of God and of Christ and will reign with him for a thousand
years* (Revelation 16:16).

If you were an artist and wanted to paint a picture
that best portrayed the meaning of hope, what would
you paint? Years ago artist George Frederic Watts titled
one of his paintings *Hope*.

It shows a woman sitting on a world that has treated her unfairly. Her eyes are bandaged, preventing her from seeing her way ahead. In her hands she holds a harp; all the strings except one are broken. Triumphantly, she strikes that last string and from it a beautiful melody buoys her spirits and fills her dark night with stars.

The Revelation sounds a note of hope as we look into the future. A person can live 40 days without food, 12 days without sleep, and six days without water. But how long can a person live without hope?

A study of hospital patients reportedly came to the conclusion that there exists a strong correlation between life expectancy and future-oriented thinking. A patient who looked ahead to upcoming events was more likely to live than one whose thinking was confined to the daily hospital routine.

This conclusion comes as no surprise. After all, God created us to dream beyond the moment. Physically, we are confined to the moment; we can't step back in time to change the past, nor can we step into the future to know what will happen next. But mentally, we have the capacity to dream of the future, to plan and to hope for things not seen.

We call it hope; the power of hope is the substance of our faith. The Bible says, "Now faith is being sure of what we hope for and certain of what we do not see" (Hebrews 11:1). Take Abraham, for example.

One night God showed him the stars of the sky and told him that his descendants would one day be as the number of the stars. Yet, at that time Abraham and Sarah were senior citizens and she was physically unable to have children. Nevertheless, "Against all hope, Abraham in hope believed and so became the father of many nations" (Romans 4:18). His vision of the future gave him hope for the moment. He even looked beyond his earthly future in the land of Canaan to his heavenly future, "for he looked for a city [with] foundations, whose builder and maker is God" (Hebrews 11:10, *KJV*).

As believers, our vision of hope is twofold. First, we believe that the quality of life here and now can always be better. We are agents of hope in a world of despair. I point this out because some have criticized our belief in the return of Christ, saying that we have a "blocked future" — a future that offers hope for eternity but no hope for the present.

In reality, the world is a better place today because of the influence of Christianity. Consider all the hospitals, drug and alcohol recovery programs, support groups, schools, universities, and social programs established by the church. And consider the moral and political action groups which keep the nation focused on Biblical values.

But we must face the fact that after we have done all we can to make our world the best place it can be, the Bible tells us in no uncertain terms that evil will continue until the end of the time (see 2 Timothy 3:1–7).

Even so, this doesn't mean that we should not work toward a better world today. We should. Those who believe in the return of Christ do not shy away from social, political and moral action. While we know that our utopia will come only when Christ sets up His kingdom, we must also assume our roles as "the light of the world" and "the salt of the earth."

Having said that, I must also emphasize that our vision of hope goes beyond better schools, spiritual revival in the culture, or an improved political situation. We have an eternal hope — the kingdom of God.

That future is bound up in one word: *Millennium* — the millennial kingdom of Christ. The return of Christ is the "blessed hope" of the world (Titus 2:13). The word *millennium* has taken on a whole new level of significance. I am writing these words as we stand on the brink of Year 2000 and a new millennium. People of all religious backgrounds and orientations are filled with wonder over what the new millennium will bring.

Many Christians are asking, "Will this be the time of the return of Christ and the establishment of His millennial kingdom?" While no one knows all that the new millennium will hold, one thing is certain: it is futile to try to predict the timing of Christ's return.

The question for us is: What does the Bible tell us about the Millennium, or the kingdom age of Christ?

LITERAL OR
SYMBOLIC?

The word *millennium* simply means "a thousand years" and is used only in Revelation 20. But Christ's Millennium is also referred to in the Bible as "the last days" (Isaiah 2:1), "the day of the Lord" (Zechariah 14:1), and "the kingdom of heaven" (Matthew 18:3). It is "the renewal of all things" (Matthew 19:28), "the restoration of all things" (Acts 3:21, *NASB*) and "the age to come" (Hebrews 6:5, *NASB*).

Is the "thousand years" a literal time period? I suppose no one knows for sure. We remember that the numbers used in Revelation seldom represent only numerical values; they represent spiritual truths as well.

The number *1,000* speaks of a golden age, a period of time during which God will fulfill His purpose to "to bring all things in heaven and on earth together under one head, even Christ" (Ephesians 1:10). In all honesty, whether or not the number 1,000 is literal or figurative doesn't really matter. What matters is the fact that Christ will rule as King of kings and we will reign with Him.

THREE
SCHOOLS OF THOUGHT

Various scholars hold to three different views on the Millennium. *Amillennialism* says that there is no literal kingdom age of Christ and that this passage simply refers to believers in heaven who now rule with Christ.

Postmillennialism presents the interpretation that the present world system will eventually be Christianized by the church's evangelistic efforts and political influences; and, as a result, a long period of peace and prosperity will ensue. According to this belief, at the conclusion of this millennium, which the church will basically create, Christ will return.

Finally, *premillennialism* (the position I hold) states that Christ will return in His glory at Armageddon to establish the kingdom of God on the earth. The early church believed in the premillennial return of Christ. Only after several centuries did these other positions begin to develop. You see, you can't have a kingdom without a king. When He comes, the kingdom will be a reality and the Lord's Prayer will finally be realized:

> *"Thy kingdom come, thy will be done on earth as it is in heaven"*
> (Matthew 6:10, *KJV*).

Our view of a perfect world is sometimes distorted, sometimes humorous. Someone said a perfect world is where:

. . . a person should feel as good at 50 as he did at 17, and he would actually be as smart at 50 as he thought he was at 17.

. . . doing what was good for you would be what you enjoyed doing the most.

. . . pro baseball players would complain about those spoiled teachers having contracts worth millions of dollars.

. . . the mail would always be early, the check would always be in the mail, and it would be written for more than you expected.

. . . potato chips might have calories, but if you ate them with dip, every one of the calories would be neutralized.

. . . if a guy from the government said to you, "I'm here to help," not only would he mean it, but he'd do it.

. . . first impressions wouldn't count for nearly as much as ultimate performance.

We are constantly seeking and striving for a world better than this. The Millennium will be a perfect world under the rule of Christ. Everything will change for the better — from the animals to agriculture, from education to economics. The quality of nature, relationships and institutions will be the quality of righteousness and peace.

IN SEARCH OF
THE MESSIAH

The portrait of the Millennium begins with the Jewish concept of the Messiah. The Millennium is essentially the messianic or kingdom age. In one sense of the word, the coming of the Messiah is the single thread interwoven through the Bible linking the Old and New Testaments.

But one thing is obvious when you read the New Testament: Jesus' concept of His messianic mission was different from the prevailing perspective of the Messiah held by the rabbis of His day.

The word *messiah* is a Greek translation of the Aramaic *mesiha*, derived from the Hebrew word *mashach*, meaning "to anoint, or to smear with oil." *Messiah* simply means the "Anointed One." The English word *Christ* comes from the Greek *Christos*, meaning "Messiah." What did Israel expect of her Messiah?

Israel's hope for a king and a kingdom was reawakened when the remnant from Babylon returned to their homeland under the leadership of Zerubbabel, a descendant of David and governor of Judah about 500 years before Christ. Even though the city of Jerusalem was rebuilt and the Temple restored, it soon became apparent that Zerubbabel was not another David.

So people began to project the possibility of Messiah's coming into the distant future. Eventually, many were disillusioned and could only envision Him coming at the end of the age.

This was the prevailing mood in Israel during the time of the prophets:

✝ Jeremiah foretold a continuation of the Davidic line (Jeremiah 33).

✝ Isaiah prophesied of the glory of the coming king (Isaiah 9:11).

✝ Micah announced the birth of the Davidic king would be in Bethlehem (Micah 5:2).

✝ Zechariah described the character of the messianic kingdom (9:12).

These prophecies were more than expressions of the people's longing for the Messiah; they sounded the prophetic voice of God. All these messianic promises were fulfilled when the angel announced to Mary the miracle of her miraculous conception:

> *"You are to give him the name Jesus. He will be great and will be called the Son of the Most High. The Lord God will give him the throne of his father David, and he will reign over the house of Jacob forever; his kingdom will never end"* (Luke 1:31–33).

Between the Testaments (called the silent years or the intertestamental period), several different ideas about the Messiah emerged which are important for us to understand. Many believed two Messiahs would appear: a Levitical Messiah who would serve as priest, and a Davidic Messiah who would rule as king. But by the time Jesus was born, most people believed that only one Messiah would come from the line of David.

What would this Davidic Messiah be like? Most pictured the Messiah as a composite of Old Testament and apocryphal descriptions. By and large, people believed that Elijah would return as the forerunner of the Messiah. The messianic age would begin with the travail of the Messiah.

The new age would be a time of terror at the Day of the Lord, a time of cosmic upheaval, and a time of complete disintegration for the universe itself and all relationships. It would be a time of divine judgment. Gentile nations would either be judged or redeemed, depending on various theological perspectives.

There would be an ingathering of Israel back to her homeland from all nations. Jerusalem would be restored and given a new Temple. The dead would be raised. The new age of the Kingdom would endure forever.

A complete restoration of all things would occur, including a reuniting of the divided kingdom; abundant agricultural fertility; the end of all war and strife; peace between man and the animal kingdom; the removal of all sickness, pain, sorrow and death; and a climax of holiness and righteousness.[1]

The majority of Jews shared the belief in the coming of a mighty Messiah-warrior of David's line. The Qumran community (where the Dead Sea Scrolls were found) and the Zealots shared this view and were eagerly waiting for Messiah to come and free them from the Roman yoke of oppression. This explains why Jesus did not refer to Himself as Messiah and discouraged others from using the title. If He had gone around telling everyone that He was the Messiah, mass hysteria would have erupted, calling for the overthrow of Rome.

Jesus knew full well that He was the Messiah and so did His disciples (Mark 8:29). But it was not until His trial before Caiaphas, the high priest, that He openly declared Himself to be the Messiah (14:61, 62).

So, the people expected the Messiah to usher in a political-military kingdom by force. Jesus, however, knew that His purpose was first to establish the kingdom of God spiritually in the hearts of all people. The kingdom of God would only come through the power of His crucifixion, resurrection and ascension.

At Caesarea Philippi, where Peter made the confession, "You are the Christ [Messiah], the Son of the living God," Jesus "warned his disciples not to tell anyone that he was the Christ" (Matthew 16:16, 20).

Furthermore, "From that time on Jesus began to explain to his disciples that he must go to Jerusalem and suffer many things . . . and that he must be killed and on the third day be raised to life"(v. 21).

Jesus knew that He could only fulfill His messianic mission by suffering for the sins of the world (Mark 10:45). But the mob rejected Him with cries of "Crucify Him!" No wonder He wept over Jerusalem shortly before His death: "You did not recognize the time of God's coming to you" (Luke 19:44). Looking for a politician, they missed the Savior.

WHERE IS
THE KINGDOM?

Into this environment, with the Jewish people longing for a Messiah to deliver them from Roman oppression and establish the Davidic kingdom of old, Jesus came.

While He deliberately avoided the title "Messiah," He spoke freely of Himself as the Son of Man, and boldly announced that by His very presence in the world, "the Kingdom of God is at hand." Announcing the kingdom, Jesus captured the attention of everyone in Israel. His kingdom message rang out as a message of hope. It struck a responsive chord with those who envisioned a empire of vast economic, political and military resources that would overthrow Rome and usher in the glory of the Davidic kingdom.

And who can blame them for having such high hopes? After all, for centuries Israel had been subject to Gentile world powers just as the prophet Daniel foresaw in his apocalyptic visions.

First, they were in bondage to Babylon (605 B.C.); then to Medo-Persia (539 B.C.); followed by Greece under Alexander the Great (333 B.C.); and now to Rome (63 B.C.). I mean, enough is enough! They wanted freedom. And rightly so.

To compound matters, Rome had placed a puppet king over Israel named Herod. He was an Edomite, not a Jew.

He looked out only for his own interests. He served the agenda of Rome, not Israel. Israel existed as a Roman territory. The Antonio Fortress, where Pilate ruled as governor, was constructed next to the Temple.

Roman authority controlled Herod and the Temple party of the Sadducees, made up of the priests. Israel was so heavily taxed that much of the land existed in abject poverty. Needless to say, it was a time of darkness—economically, socially, politically and, most of all, spiritually. The people longed for Isaiah's Messiah to come.

When Jesus announced, "The kingdom of heaven is here!" it was to a hopeless and desperate people. No wonder they flocked by the multitudes to hear Him. But when they asked Him when His kingdom would come and how it would appear, He made a most unusual statement:

> *"The kingdom of God does not come with your careful observation, nor will people say, 'Here it is,' or 'There it is,' because the kingdom of God is within you"* (Luke 17:20, 21).

His kingdom would not come with military might, political power or religious aristocracy. His kingdom would not be measured by lands conquered, subjects and slaves, wealth and power. His kingdom would not be centered in the holy city of Jerusalem, on the seven hills of Rome, or in the cradle of Babylon.

His kingdom would be established in the hearts of everyone who believed in Him: "To all who received him, to those who believed in his name, he gave the right to become children of God" (John 1:12). The Greek word for kingdom, *basileia*, means "the rule of God; the sphere of God's rule." It is located wherever the king rules. As such, it is not bound by time, space and matter. Nor is it limited to geographical boundaries.

E. Stanley Jones said, "The kingdom of God is God's total answer for man's total need." This explains the kingdom here and now, but what about the kingdom then and there?

PARADISE
REGAINED

The millennial kingdom of Christ is actually the fulfillment of the covenant God made with David. God promised David three things: a *house*, a *kingdom* and a *throne* for his descendants throughout eternity. All of this is fulfilled in Jesus.

The Old Testament prophets viewed the eternal throne of David as the Messiah's throne (see Jeremiah 23:5, 6; 30:8, 9; 33:14-17, 20-21; Ezekiel 37:24, 25; Daniel 7:13, 14; Amos 9:11). Isaiah's prophecy of the Messiah's kingdom is without question the fulfillment of God's covenant with David:

> *For unto us a child is born, unto us a son is given: and the government shall be upon his shoulder: and his name shall be called Wonderful, Counsellor, The mighty God, The everlasting Father, The Prince of Peace. Of the increase of his government and peace there shall be no end, upon the throne of David, and upon his kingdom, to order it, and to establish it with judgment and with justice from henceforth even for ever. The zeal of the Lord of hosts will perform this* (Isaiah 9:6, 7, KJV).

What will Christ's Millennium be like? First of all, Jesus will rule over all the world, and His people will reign with Him. Zechariah put it this way: "The Lord will be king over the whole earth. On that day there will be one Lord, and his name the only name" (14:9).

In John's apocalyptic vision, the seventh trumpet announces the Millennium:

> *The seventh angel sounded his trumpet, and there were loud voices in heaven, which said: "The kingdom of the world has become the kingdom of our Lord and of his Christ, and he will reign for ever and ever"* (Revelation 11:15).

This is why I said earlier that you cannot have a kingdom without a king. John also tells us that we will reign with Christ: "They. . . reigned with Christ for a thousand years" (20:4). When John says that the martyrs come to life to reign with Christ, he is using the martyrs to represent all believers. Jesus promises us a place of rulership: "To him who overcomes, I will give the right to sit with me on my throne, just as I overcame and sat down with my Father on his throne" (3:21). He also told the Twelve that they would rule over the 12 tribes of Israel (Luke 22:29, 30).

Two words are used many times in Scripture to describe world conditions in the Millennium: *righteousness* and *peace*.

First, Satan will be bound in the Abyss during the Lord's Millennium:

> *And I saw an angel coming down out of heaven, having the key to the Abyss and holding in his hand a great chain. He seized the dragon, that ancient serpent, who is the devil, or Satan, and bound him for a thousand years. He threw him into the Abyss, and locked and sealed it over him, to keep him from deceiving the nations anymore until the thousand years were ended. After that, he must be set free for a short time* (Revelation 20:1-3).

Peace will be the order of the day. Wars will cease. Famines will disappear. Ecological disturbances will end. Jerusalem will be established again as the city of God. All people will worship the true and living God, and Jesus Christ as Lord (15:4). It will be a time of unparalleled, worldwide prosperity. Talk about the good life! Isaiah describes the world to come:

In the last days the mountain of the Lord's temple will be established as chief among the mountains; it will be raised above the hills, and all nations will stream to it.

Many peoples will come and say, "Come, let us go up to the mountain of the Lord, to the house of the God of Jacob. He will teach us his ways, so that we may walk in his paths." The law will go out from Zion, the word of the Lord from Jerusalem. He will judge between the nations and will settle disputes for many peoples. They will beat their swords into plowshares and their spears into pruning hooks. Nation will not take up sword against nation, nor will they train for war anymore.

Come, O house of Jacob, let us walk in the light of the Lord (Isaiah 2:2-5).

Later, Isaiah catches another glimpse of the Messiah's kingdom:

The wolf will live with the lamb, the leopard will lie down with the goat, the calf and the lion and the yearling together; and a little child will lead them. The cow will feed with the bear, their young will lie down together, and the lion will eat straw like the ox. The infant will play near the hole of the cobra, and the young child put his hand into the viper's nest. They will neither harm nor destroy on all my holy mountain, for the earth will be full of the knowledge of the Lord as the waters cover the sea (11:6–9).

Tragically, John goes on to tell us that this beautiful age of peace and prosperity will end with a final rebellion. When the thousand years are over, Satan will be released from his prison and will go out to deceive the nations in the four corners of the earth—Gog and Magog—to gather them for battle.

The number of people will be like the sand on the seashore. The terms *Gog* and *Magog* are taken from Ezekiel 38 and 39 to describe an army in rebellion to God. They will march across the breadth of the earth and surround the camp of God's people. But fire will come down from heaven and devour them.

Then the devil will be thrown into the lake of fire, where the Beast and the False Prophet had been thrown (see Revelation 20:7-10). Even the psalmist foresaw this rebellion:

> *Why do the nations conspire and the peoples plot in vain? The kings of the earth take their stand and the rulers gather together against the Lord and against his Anointed One. "Let us break their chains," they say, "and throw off their fetters."*
>
> *The One enthroned in heaven laughs; the Lord scoffs at them. Then he rebukes them in his anger and terrifies them in his wrath, saying, "I have installed my King on Zion, my holy hill"* (Psalm 2:1-6).

The good news is that the enemies of God will meet certain judgment. The sudden destruction of Gog and Magog reminds us that the victory Christ won at Calvary will be enforced in one terrifying moment. *My point is that the victory will not have to be won — it has already been won on the Cross.* The fact that this rebellion will occur at the end of the Millennium teaches us a vital lesson for our own lives.

Think of this — even with the perfect environmental conditions of the Millennium, rebellion and sin can still occur. The human heart must first be transformed. That's why Jesus said the Kingdom is within you, not just around you.

When Satan is loosed, many will yield to his temptations and rebel against God. Lasting change will never come to our world simply through judicial, economic, or social reforms; a spiritual reform is needed — the change of the human heart where Christ reigns as Lord.

In March 1990, Republican Party chairman Lee Atwater was diagnosed with an inoperable brain tumor. Before his death, Atwater — who began writing apology notes to many political enemies—told columnist Cal Thomas, "I have found Jesus Christ. It's that simple. He's made a difference, and I'm glad I've found Him while there's still time."

The month Atwater turned 40, eaten up with cancer, he said:

> The '80s were about acquiring—wealth, power, prestige. I know. I acquired more wealth, power and prestige than most. But you can acquire all you want and still feel empty. What power wouldn't I trade for a little more time with my family? What price wouldn't I pay for an evening with friends? It took a deadly illness to put me eye to eye with that truth, but it is a truth that the country, caught up in its ruthless ambitions and moral decay, can learn on my dime. I don't know who will lead us through the '90s, but they must be made to speak to this spiritual vacuum at the heart of American society, this tumor of the soul."[2]

CAN WE TAKE THAT
OUT OF THE BIBLE?

Have you ever read something in the Bible and wished it weren't there? I have. It may surprise you that I would be so honest, but it's true. When I read the description of the Great White Throne Judgment that will take place after the Millennium, my heart trembles. This is the most troubling passage in the entire Bible:

> *Then I saw a great white throne and him who was seated on it. Earth and sky fled from his presence, and there was no place for them. And I saw the dead, great and small, standing before the throne, and books were opened. Another book was opened, which is the book of life. The dead were judged according to what they had done as recorded in the books. . . . Then death and Hades were thrown into the lake of fire. The lake of fire is the second*

*death. If anyone's name was not found written in the book of
life, he was thrown into the lake of fire* (Revelation 20:11-15).

The concept of judgment doesn't set too well with modern thinkers. However, a surprising number of people believe in hell. A recent Gallup Poll indicated that 73 percent
of American adults believe in hell. Seventy-one percent believe the devil exists. But the closer people get to dying, the
percentage of people who believe in hell decreases.[3]

Several questions come to mind when we think about
the final judgment. First, who will be judged at the Great
White Throne? The Revelator sees those who have rebelled
against God and rejected His Word and His Son Jesus Christ.
What will be the criteria for judgment?

John tells us that they will be judged "according to what
they had done." This means *how* they will be judged by the
way they responded with their own conscience to the knowledge of truth they have (Romans 2:14, 15), to the law of
God (1 John 3:4), to the person of Christ (John 3:17, 18;
12:48); and by the way they lived their lives (Matthew 12:36;
2 Corinthians 5:10).

But your eternal destiny boils down to only one issue: Is
your name written in the Lamb's Book of Life? That's all
that really matters. We read about the Book of Life in many
places in the Bible (see Exodus 32:33; Daniel 12:1; Luke 10:20;
Revelation 3:5; 21:27).

"How do I get my name written in it?" you may be asking. By simply accepting Jesus Christ as the Son of God, by
repenting of your sins, and by confessing Him as Lord of
your life.

*If you confess with your mouth, 'Jesus is Lord,' and believe in
your heart that God raised him from the dead, you will be saved.
For it is with your heart that you believe and are justified, and*

it is with your mouth that you confess and are saved (Romans 10:9, 10).

You can accept Christ right now. Pray and ask God to forgive you of your sins. Ask Christ Jesus to come and live in your heart. Pledge Him your life and your future. Confess that Jesus Christ is Lord of your life from this moment on and God will work the incredible miracle of salvation. You will be a new creation—old things will pass away and everything will become new!

What will happen to those whose names are not written in the Book of Life? Horribly and tragically, John sees them thrown into the lake of fire.

I will be the first to admit that I don't understand everything there is to know about eternal judgment, about hell and this place called the lake of fire. The Bible does tell us that hell was prepared for the devil and his angels and that it is a place of outer darkness, weeping and gnashing of teeth, and eternal fire.

Most importantly, we know beyond a shadow of doubt that God is merciful and that He will judge people only to the level of their accountability and the light of knowledge they have. When your heart gets troubled about where people go after they die, remember God's blessed promise in Genesis 18:25: "Will not the Judge of all the earth do right?" We answer unequivocally, "Yes!"

Enough bad news—here's the good news: You don't have to face judgment. That's why Jesus died for us. On the cross He took our judgment that we might be forgiven and pardoned (see 2 Corinthians 5:21). We have confidence that on the Day of Judgment He will say to us, "Well done, good and faithful servant. Enter into the kingdom prepared for you since the world began!" (see Matthew 25:23, 34).

START
REIGNING TODAY

All this talk about reigning with Christ in eternity is great, but you can start reigning in life today. You don't have to wait until the Millennium to reign. The apostle Paul tells us, "How much more will those who receive God's abundant provision of grace and of the gift of righteousness *reign in life* through the one man, Jesus Christ" (Romans 5:17, emphasis mine).

In Christ, you can reign over sin, depression, fear and problems, because "you, dear children, are from God and have overcome them, because the one who is in you is greater than the one who is in the world" (1 John 4:4).

What does it take to reign in life? Remember the qualities of the millennial kingdom: righteousness and peace. This is what Paul says about living in the Kingdom here, and now: "For the kingdom of God is . . . a matter of . . . righteousness, peace and joy in the Holy Spirit" (Romans 14:17).

With His righteousness, peace and joy, you can overcome every difficulty you face. The Kingdom life starts today.

As Jesus said, "The Kingdom is within you!"

Chapter
11

They sit at the Feet—
they hear the Word—
they see how truly the Promise
runs.
They have cast their burden upon the
Lord. . . .

(Rudyard Kipling, "The Sons of Martha")

A NEW HEAVEN,
A NEW EARTH

*Then I saw a new heaven and a new earth,
for the first heaven and the first earth had
passed away, and there was no longer any
sea.* (Revelation 4:1, 2).

B ishop Fulton Sheen tells of speaking one night
at Town Hall in Philadelphia. He decided to
walk from his hotel, even though he was unfamiliar
with the city. Sure enough, he got lost and stopped to ask
some boys playing in the street how to get there.

One of the boys asked him, "What are you going to do
there?"

The bishop replied, "I'm going to give a talk."

"About what?" the little fellow inquired.

"I'm going to give a talk about how to get to heaven.
Would you like to come along and listen?"

"Are you kidding?" said the boy. "You don't even know how to get to Town Hall!"

Perhaps the most important question we ask at some time in our lives is, "What is heaven, and how do we get there?" Strikingly, nearly 80 percent of Americans believe in life after death, and two-thirds are certain there is a heaven.

As we turn to the Bible for our answer, we are introduced to the term *heaven* right up front: "In the beginning God created the heavens and the earth." Not only that, the Bible ends with a magnificent portrait of a new heaven and a new earth.

The Bible uses the term *heaven* three ways. *First,* there is the natural atmosphere that surrounds the earth.

Second, there is the heavenly realm or the supernatural realm of angels and demons. For instance, Ephesians mentions "the heavenly realm" five times. It says we are seated with Christ in the heavenly realms and that we struggle against evil forces in the heavenly realms (2:6, 6:12).

Third, the term *heaven* is used for the dwelling place of God and for the saints and angels. Once Paul talked about being caught up to the third heaven (2 Corinthians 12:2). Jesus spoke often of the kingdom of heaven and told us in no uncertain terms of its reality (John 14:1-3).

Perhaps the greatest insight into heaven and the hope we have of eternal life is found in Revelation 21 and 22. Here John the apostle experiences his final vision on the island of Patmos.

John was exiled on Patmos "because of the word of God and the testimony of Jesus" (1:9) between A.D. 94 and 96.

The church itself was being persecuted by the government of Rome, and many were losing hope and were terrified for their lives. The Revelation was given to John so he could encourage the church to see life and their sufferings from an eternal perspective.

Here are some of the lessons we have learned on our journey through the Revelation:

1. *Jesus Christ is Lord.* The book is the revelation of Jesus Christ, the Son of God and the Son of Man. He is both Lamb of God and Lion of the tribe of Judah. He is Savior and Lord . . . suffering Servant and conquering King.

2. *God is sovereign.* The throne of God appears 45 times—in every chapter except 2, 8 and 9. John calls God "the Almighty," which means the One who controls all things. Because God is sovereign, all of heaven sings in praise, "Hallelujah! For our Lord God Almighty reigns" (19:6).

3. *Spiritual warfare is real.* The church fulfills its mission in the world to preach the gospel against five enemies: the Dragon, who is the devil; the Antichrist; the False Prophet; the mark of the Beast; and Mystery Babylon the Great, which represents political persecution of God's people.

Today these are spiritual forces, but during the Great Tribulation they will be actual personalities and a system of global economy.

4. *The church is triumphant.* In spite of every attempt by the devil to hinder the gospel, the people of God overcome him by the blood of the Lamb and by the word of their testimony. John sees the redeemed standing with Christ on Mount Zion because they overcame the Beast, his image, and the number of his name.

Revelation's triumphant promise confirms Romans 8:37: "We are more than conquerors through him who loved us."

5. *The future belongs to God.* While no one can fully comprehend the eternal plan of God, the Bible reveals that the future will include the rapture of the church; the Great Tribulation; Armageddon and the second coming of Christ; the Millennium; the Great White Throne Judgment; and, ultimately, a new heaven and a new earth, the home of righteousness.

The 54 uses of the number *seven* in the book represent the fact that God will complete what He started at the Creation. John's last and greatest vision is a glimpse of eternity with God. Listen to his account:

> One of the seven angels . . . said to me, 'Come, I will show you the bride, the wife of the Lamb.' And he carried me away in the Spirit to a mountain great and high, and showed me the Holy City, Jerusalem, coming down out of heaven from God (Revelation 21:9, 10).

Paul assured us, "No eye has seen, no ear has heard, no mind has conceived what God has prepared for those who love him"—now for the rest of the story—"*but God has revealed it to us by his Spirit.* The Spirit searches all things, even the deep things of God" (1 Corinthians 2:9, 10). Likewise, John shows us what God has revealed about eternity.

How do you picture heaven? Some have unrealistic expectations. They remind me of the story of a single man and woman who were friends for many years. They liked each other but never dated. Both died and ran into each other in heaven.

After renewing their friendship in heaven, they went to Saint Peter and told him they wanted to get married. "Take your time and think about it," Saint Peter said.

"You have all eternity to be together. Come back and see me about it in 50 years."

Fifty years passed and the couple returned. Again they told Peter they wanted to get married.

"Take your time and think about it some more," Saint Peter said. "Come back and see me in another 50 years. If we don't have a preacher up here by then, I'll marry you myself."

A NEW
CREATION

The Bible ends the way it begins — affirming the fact that God is our Creator. We are not here by an evolutionary accident; we are made in the image of God. Notice the fact that heaven and earth are one. The Lord's Prayer has been fulfilled, "Thy will be done on earth as it is in heaven." The rule of heaven is now the rule of earth. The Bible begins with the act of Creation and ends with a new creation.

Isaiah saw this new creation:

> Behold, I will create new heavens and a new earth. The former things will not be remembered, nor will they come to mind. But be glad and rejoice forever in what I will create, for I will create Jerusalem to be a delight and its people a joy (Isaiah 65:17, 18).

He also sees it as a place where life is a continual act of worship (see 66:22, 23).

The apostle Peter tells us, "That day [the day of God] will bring about the destruction of the heavens by fire, and the elements will melt in the heat. But in keeping with his promise we are looking forward to a new heaven and a new earth, the home of righteousness" (2 Peter 3:12, 13).

The exciting promise is that we will receive new, glorified bodies (1 Corinthians 15:51-55; Philippians 3:21).

John makes an intriguing observation about this new creation: "There was no more sea." What does he mean when he says there will be no more seas on the new earth? Well, he may simply mean that the new earth will have a diminishing of the seas. But there may also be a spiritual meaning.

Two seas are mentioned in Revelation: the sea out of which the Antichrist rises and on which Mystery Babylon sits (13:1; 17:1) and the sea of glass before the throne of God, around which the redeemed declare the triumph of the Lamb (15:2).

The restless sea of humanity (see Isaiah 57:20) is probably the figure being used here. In ancient times, the seas were frightening to the people. They represented chaos, storms and upheaval. When Jesus Christ returns and establishes the kingdom of God, all the chaos in the world caused by the presence of evil will vanish, and the peace of God will be the order of the day, and will govern every aspect of life.

THE HEAVENLY
NEW JERUSALEM

No vision of the future would be complete without a final chapter on the destiny of Israel in the plan of God. The history of Jerusalem is rich in every way. It was founded by David as the capital of the nation after he became king.

Jerusalem means "the city of peace." The name dates back to the time of Abraham when he paid tithes to the king of Salem. Jerusalem is also called the city of God (see Psalm 48:1, 2).

The image of earthly Jerusalem serves to remind us of a heavenly Jerusalem. "But the Jerusalem that is from above is free, and she is our mother" (Galatians 4:26). Paul was contrasting Mount Sinai (the law) with Jerusalem (grace) in this verse.

We worship in the heavenly Jerusalem: "But you have come to Mount Zion, to the heavenly Jerusalem, the city of the living God. You have come to thousands upon thousands of angels in joyful assembly, to the church of the firstborn, whose names are written in heaven" (Hebrews 12:22, 23).

What else does John see in this heavenly Jerusalem, the "Holy City"? The Bible has 1,200 references to cities; 119 different ones are mentioned. John's vision contains elements of Jerusalem, the Temple, and the Garden of Eden. Perhaps Abraham was the first human to see this city (see Hebrews 11:10).

The heavenly Jerusalem is contrasted with the city of Babylon in the Revelation. Babylon will be a city of chaos and strife, ruled by the antichrist spirit. That city will fall but New Jerusalem is the Holy City and will endure forever. Unbelievable, magnificent beauty features this city where we will live eternally.

What will the New Jerusalem be like? As John is carried away by the Spirit to a great, high mountain, he gets a closer look (21:9, 10). The city radiates with the glory of God, a glory as clear as crystal. The 12 gates of the city, each made of a single pearl, bear the names of the 12 tribes of Israel.

The 12 foundations, each made of a precious jewel, are inscribed with the names of the 12 apostles. References to the tribes of Israel and the apostles of Christ represent all the people of God from both Old and New Testament times. The jewels of the foundations remind us of the jewels worn on the breastplate of the high priest. The eight stones in John's list are the same as those on the breastplate.

Another interesting aspect of these stones comes from an ancient Eastern myth that connected the city of the gods with the signs of the zodiac. The stones John saw are the same as those corresponding with the zodiac — with one interesting exception.

The order in the Revelation is the reverse of the order of the stones associated with the zodiac. It is as though God is saying to all the astrologers, "You've got it figured out wrong!" Indeed it is futile to try to chart your future by the stars. Chart your course by the direction of the Lord in your own heart. The future belongs to God, and so do you.

Next, the angel measures the city with a golden rod, just as Ezekiel saw in his vision of the New Jerusalem (see Ezekiel 48). The city is 12,000 stadia cubed, which is about 1,500 miles. This gives the city a total area of 2,250,000 square miles. To put it in perspective, the city would stretch from New York to London. The point is that there is room for everyone in the city.

Earlier, the temple was measured for its protection (see Revelation 11). Here, measurements are taken in order to describe the incredible beauty and magnificent size of the city. Note also that the walls are 144 cubits, or 200 feet, thick. Again we see the numerology of 12 and its multiples depicting the complete number of the people of God.

The most widely known part of his vision is the street of pure gold: "The great street of the city was of pure gold, like transparent glass" (21:21). It appears to function as the main thoroughfare of traffic for all who live there.

Then John sees the river of the water of life flowing from the throne of God (22:1). The river represents the life-giving power of the Holy Spirit (see John 7:37-39). Along the banks of the river is the Tree of Life bearing 12 kinds of fruit every month. He says "the leaves of the tree are for the healing of the nations" (22:2). Earlier he sees the nations of the world bring their glory into the city. We are reminded of God's love for all nations. Even the commission of the church is to "make disciples of all nations" (Matthew 28:19).

The greatest statement of all is that the throne of God will be in the city, and His servants will serve Him: "They will see his face" (22:4). What a fantastic thought that we will see the Father, the Son and the Holy Spirit face-to-face. That means we will enjoy full fellowship with Him. And John reminds us that when we see Him, we will be like Him (1 John 3:2).

PERPETUAL
PRAISE

The statement "His servants will serve him" (22:3) means that we will be caught up in holy worship. A.W. Tozer once referred to worship as the missing jewel of the modern church. The word *worship* simply means "worthship." It denotes the worthiness of a person who is the recipient of special honor. As creatures, we declare the glory of the Creator. Who is worthy of our praise? Is the earth worthy? Has the soil given us life?

Are the stars worthy? Shall they guide our course?

Is science worthy? Will it save us from destruction and solve all our problems?

Is government—Big Brother—our source of security?

Is religion worthy? Can we through our creeds and good deeds atone for our sins?

Is man worthy? Is he really the measure of all things?

Only God is worthy of our worship. Worship is simply

our response of love to the love of God. Heaven is a place of joyful worship, and the earth should be, too.

As important as all of these wonderful features are, it is equally impressive to see what will *not* be present in the New Jerusalem:

✝ There will be no more sorrow, for God will wipe every tear from their eyes.

✝ There will be no more curse; for death, mourning, crying and pain will cease.

✝ There will be no more conflict for the nations will walk by the light of that city and bring their splendor into it.

✝ There will be no temple, for the Lord God Almighty and the Lamb are its temple.

✝ There will be no need of the sun and moon, for the glory of God gives it light and the Lamb himself is its lamp.

✝ There will be no more night, so the gates are never shut.

✝ There will be no more sin, for the angel told John, "Nothing impure will ever enter it, nor will anyone who does what is shameful or deceitful, but only those whose names are written in the Lamb's book of life" (21:27).

Who will live in the New Jerusalem? Only the covenant people of God. The New Jerusalem is not only a city, it is a people. Our citizenship is in this heavenly city (see Philippians 3:20). In the Old Testament Israel is called the wife of Jehovah.

In the New Testament, the church is called, among other things, the bride of Christ. But here is the best news of all: "Now the dwelling of God is with men, and he will live with them" (Revelation 21:3).

In the Old Testament, the patriarchs walked with God. Moses saw His back at Sinai (Exodus 33:22, 23); Solomon saw God's glory fill the temple (2 Chronicles 7:1).

In the New Testament, God came to us incarnate in Jesus, and He now gives us the indwelling Holy Spirit so that our bodies become His temple.

But the day is coming when God and man will live together in unbroken communion as they did in Eden. We will walk with Him in the cool of the day because the old order of things will pass away and God will make all things new! The language of the covenant is used here in Revelation: "They will be his people, and God himself will be with them and be their God. . . . He who overcomes will inherit all this, and I will be his God and he will be my son" (21:3, 7).

Over and over, God tells us "I will," because He loves us with an everlasting, unfailing and undying love. Truly, as Paul said, eye has not seen, ear has not heard, neither has it entered into the heart of man what God has prepared for those who love Him.

The covenant people, like the city, are *holy*. That's the one word that describes the people of God. To be holy is to be different, special and dedicated to God for His purpose.

The Bible is called holy because it is different from other books. The tithe is called holy because it is different from other money. The priests were called holy because they were different from other men. The Sabbath is called holy because it is different from other days.

The people of God are called holy because they are different from the world — not in the sense of being weird, but in the sense of being dedicated to living for the glory of God wherever they go and whatever they do.

Betty Wein retells an old tale she heard from Elie Wiesel. A just man comes to Sodom hoping to save the city. He pickets. What else can he do? He goes from street to street, from marketplace to marketplace, shouting, "Men and women, repent. What you are doing is wrong. It will kill you; it will destroy you."

They laugh, but he goes on shouting, until one day a child stops him.

"Poor stranger, don't you see it's useless?"

"Yes," the man replies.

"Then why do you go on?" the child asks.

"At first I was convinced that I would change them. Now I go on shouting because I don't want them to change me."[1]

That's holiness. If only I had the words to communicate with you just a glimpse of what God has planned for us.

Norman Vincent Peale related the story of Thomas Edison's death as told to him by Mrs. Edison. As the great inventor lay on his deathbed, just at the edge between life and death, he struggled as if to say something. The physician leaned over him and heard him say, "It is very beautiful over there."

WHEN
HE RETURNS

The future of the world rests on the promise of Jesus to return. Three times in the closing words of the Revelation, Jesus says, "I am coming soon!" And with these three announcements the Lord of the church calls us to action.

Blessed is he who keeps the words of this prophecy (22:7). This means to treasure the words of the Revelation in your heart. Keep them safe. They are trustworthy and true. Believe the prophecies and obey the command to patient endurance and faithfulness.

My reward is with me **(22:12).** Maybe that's what kept Paul the apostle going through all his trials and imprisonments. His last words tell us that he was looking for his reward. From a lonely dungeon in Rome he wrote,

> *I have fought the good fight, I have finished the race, I have kept the faith. Now there is in store for me the crown of righteousness, which the Lord, the righteous Judge, will award to me on that day — and not only to me, but also to all who have longed for his appearing* (2 Timothy 4:7, 8).

For the third time, Jesus gives us His personal promise: "Yes, I am coming soon" (22:20).

When Douglas MacArthur left the Philippines at the beginning of World War II, he walked out into the sea to board the landing boat. Turning back to the frightened people of the island, he said assuredly, "I will return." His promise gave them hope.

We have a greater general, the captain of our salvation, who tells us in the midst of a troubled world, "I will return." No wonder John erupts in joyful praise, "Amen. Come, Lord Jesus."

THE FINAL INVITATION
" C O M E ! "

The Revelation is a book of action. Every vision, every scene in its unfolding drama, calls for a response on our part. How fitting then, for the book to end with a personal invitation from Christ.

What does He say to each one of us?

> *The Spirit and the bride say, "Come!" And let him who hears*
> *say, "Come!" Whoever is thirsty, let him come; and whoever*
> *wishes, let him take the free gift of the water of life* (22:17).

The Spirit and the Bride say, "Come." This simply means that the church and the Holy Spirit minister together, calling the world to come to Christ and be saved. An old German adage says, "The main business is to keep the main business the main business." And the main business of the church is to give the world hope in Christ.

Each of the Gospel writers exercised care in closing out their writings with the final commission of Christ to His church. Matthew recorded Him saying, "Go, and make disciples of all nations" (28:19).

Mark noted, "Go into all the world and preach the good news to all creation" (Mark 16:15).

Luke reported, "You will be my witnesses . . . to the ends of the earth" (Acts 1:8).

John portrayed Christ on the Resurrection morning declaring to a huddled group of terrified disciples, "Peace be with you! As the Father has sent me, I am sending you" (20:21).

Chuck Colson, in his book *The Body*, points out that the modern church in America has lost the focus of its mission. He issues a solemn challenge:

> So, while the church may seem to be experiencing a season
> of growth and prosperity, it is failing to move people to
> commitment and sacrifice. The hard truth is that we have
> substituted an institutionalized religion for the life-
> changing dynamic of a living faith. . . . When compared
> with previous generations of believers, we seem among

the most thoroughly at peace with our culture, the least adept at transforming society and the most desperate for a meaningful faith. Our *raison d'etre* is confused, our mission obscured, and our existence as a people in jeopardy.[2]

The word *evangelism* means the announcement of good news—the good news of God in Jesus Christ. Evangelism is not the announcement of an idea, a system or a principle; but rather, a Person. Hence, Mark's Gospel begins with the statement, "The beginning of the gospel about Jesus Christ, the Son of God" (Mark 1:1).

Rather than being coerced, forced or manipulated, evangelism springs naturally from the believer's heart that overflows with the love of God for the world (Romans 5:5). Evangelism, then, can be defined as the outflowing of the inner life.

E. Stanley Jones once said that the Holy Spirit is like electricity—He never goes in where He can't come out! That reminds me of the story of a little boy who came home from Sunday school a bit troubled and said to his mother, "Mommy, my Sunday school teacher told me today that if I invite Jesus into my heart He will come in there and live in me."

His mother replied, "That's right, sweetheart, He will."

With a look of concern the boy said, "But Mom, won't a lot of Him stick out?" That's evangelism. A lot of Jesus sticks out of us.

Then the Revelator says, "Let him who hears say, 'Come!'" Those who respond to the glorious gospel by believing on Jesus Christ are now commissioned to share their faith.

Every believer is an ambassador of Christ to share the message of God's reconciling love with the world. This is what Paul the apostle had in mind when he said, "We are therefore Christ's ambassadors, as though God were making his appeal through us" (2 Corinthians 5:20).

An ambassador is a messenger and a representative. Specifically, the ambassador is one who . . .

✝ Is *mature*, having the advantage of experience

✝ Is *responsible*, not just for his own word but also for the word of another whom he serves

✝ Is *commissioned* to bring hostile people into the kingdom or nation he represents

✝ Is *never ashamed* to implore because of the nobility of his calling

✝ Is *representing another* in name and authority.

Just as the Roman ambassador, whom Paul had in mind, spoke with the full authority of the emperor himself, so we, too, speak in the full authority of the name of Jesus Christ. Whenever we share the message of Christ, great things happen for the kingdom of God.

The largest crowd Charles Spurgeon addressed came the night he spoke in the Crystal Palace to a crowd of 23,654 people. A mutiny had occurred in India protesting Britain's rule over that land, and a service of national humiliation was planned. Spurgeon was selected to deliver the sermon.

He went to the Crystal Palace the night before the service to test the acoustics, since the building had not been constructed with religious services in mind. As Spurgeon stood on the platform, he repeated the verse, "Behold the Lamb of God which takes away the sin of the world."

His words were heard by a man working somewhere in the building. The man came to Spurgeon several days later to say that those words had touched his heart. That night alone in the Crystal Palace he received Jesus Christ.[3]

Finally, the invitation reads, "Whoever is thirsty, let him come; and whoever wishes, let him take the free gift of the water of life." The message is clear — you can have life . . . real life . . . abundant life. And the cost is free.

As the ancient prophet said, "Come, all you who are thirsty, come to the waters; and you who have no money, come, buy and eat! Come, buy wine and milk without money and without cost" (Isaiah 55:1).

The word *come* may be the most important word in the entire Bible, because it is God's word of invitation. God will not force anyone to repent of their sins, to believe in Christ, or even to love and obey Him. God loves us unconditionally. He has provided for our salvation as a free gift based on the death, burial, resurrection and ascension of Jesus Christ.

He has sent the Holy Spirit, who convicts us of our sins, calls us to Christ, and gives us the gift of faith so that we can respond. But He leaves the final decision up to us. Max Lucado reminds us, "If there are a thousand steps between us and God, He will take all but one. He will leave the final one for us. The choice is ours." When we make the right choice the gift we receive is eternal life.

An English postal clerk, whose job was to handle letters that were inadequately addressed, sat at his desk on Christmas Eve. He was brokenhearted because death had taken his little son. He was given a letter addressed in childlike writing to *"Santa Claus, The North Pole."* Attached to it was a note from a postman, giving the address where he had picked up the letter.

The clerk was startled because it was his own address. The writing was that of his daughter. The letter read:

Dear Santa,

We're very sad at our house this year. My little brother went to heaven last week. You need not give me anything. But if you could give Daddy something that would make him stop crying, I wish you would. I heard him say to Mommy that only eternity can cure him. Could you send him some of that?"[4]

Have you responded to the King's invitation to drink of the water of life freely — to receive Jesus Christ as your Savior and Lord?

When you do, you are heir to the greatest of all inheritances — eternal life!

ENDNOTES

Chapter 1

[1]*The National and International Religion Report* Dec. 25, 1995.

[2]Robert D. Kaplan, "The Coming Anarchy," *The Atlantic Monthly* Feb. 1994: 44-76.

[3]Gayle White, "A Christian world by 2000?," *The Atlanta Journal-Constitution,* Jan. 3, 1998: D1.

Chapter 2

[1]Larry Burkett, "Y2K: a 'real and serious' threat," *Money Matters* June 1998: 1.

[2]J. Daryl Charles, "An Apocalyptic Tribute to the Lamb," *Journal of the Evangelical Theological Society*, Vol. 34, No. 4, Dec. 1991: 461.

[3]Jeffrey L. Sheler, "The Christmas Covenant," *U.S. News & World Report* Dec. 19, 1994: 62.

[4]John F. Walvoord, *The Rapture Question* (Grand Rapids: Zondervan, 1979) 182.

[5]Walvoord, 51.

[6]J. Dwight Pentecost, *Things to Come* (Grand Rapids: Zondervan, rep. ed., 1964) 241.

[7]Thomas D. Webster, "Sir Matthew Hale: A Man of Integrity," *Decision* Feb. 1996: 10.

[8]Billy Graham, *World Aflame* (Garden City, NJ: Double-day, 1965) 249.

[9]*The Pastor's Weekly Bulletin* Sept. 30, 1994: 1.

[10]*Decision* Jan. 1996: 30.

Chapter 3

[1]Paul S. Rees, *Triumphant in Trouble* (Westwood, NJ: Fleming H. Revell Co., 1962) 35, 36.

[2]Andrés Tapia, "Reaching the First Post-Christian Generation," *Christianity Today* Sept. 12, 1994: 19.

[3]Same.

[4]Arnold Dallimore, *Spurgeon* (Chicago: Moody Press, 1984) 94.

[5]Corrie ten Boom, *Tramp for the Lord* (Old Tappan, NJ: Fleming H. Revell, 1974) 12.

[6]Dietrich Bonhoeffer, *The Cost of Discipleship* (New York: McMillan Publishing Co., 1963) 45-48.

[7]Peg Rankin, *Yet Will I Trust Him* (Ventura, CA: Regal Books, 1983) 54.

[8]Harolan Papov, *Tortured for His Faith* (Grand Rapids: Zondervan, 1970) 45.

Chapter 4

[1]Quoted in *Pulpit Helps* Mar. 1994: 16.

Chapter 5

[1]Alex Buchan, "Signs and Wonders in China," *Charisma* Jan. 1998: 40–41.

[2]Quoted in *Bits and Pieces* Jan. 18, 1998: 22-23.

Chapter 6

[1]Erwin Lutzer, *You're Richer Than You Think* (Wheaton, IL: Victor Books, 1979) 9.

Chapter 8

[1]Told by Billy Graham, "New Heart, New Beginning," *Decision* Jan. 1997: 2.

Chapter 9

[1]Jeffrey L. Sheler, "The Christmas Covenant," *U.S. News & World Report* Dec. 19, 1994: 62-64.

[2]Sheler, 62-64.

[3]Frank E. Gaebelein, ed., *The Expositor's Bible Commentary* Vol. 12 (Grand Rapids: Zondervan, 1981) 550, 551.

[4]Gaebelein, 552.

[5]William Barclay, *The Revelation of John* Vol. 2 (Philadelphia: The Westminster Press, 1976) 181.

Chapter 10

[1]William Barclay, *Jesus As They Saw Him* (Grand Rapids: Eerdmans, 1962) 111-152.

[2]Patrick Morely, "Finding Success That Matters," *The Christian Businessman* Apr. 1998: 48, 49.

[3]*The Atlanta Journal-Constitution* Aug. 17, 1996: D1.

Chapter 11

[1]Craig B. Larson, ed., *Illustrations for Preaching & Teaching* (Grand Rapids: Baker Books, 1993) 109.

[2]Chuck Colson, *The Body* (Dallas: Word Publishing, 1992) 31.

[3]Donald N. Bowdle, *Redemption Accomplished and Applied* (Cleveland, TN: Pathway Press, 1972) 109, 110.

[4]Arnold Dallimore, *Spurgeon* (Chicago: Moody Press, 1984) 95.

[5]Told by Billy Graham in *Decision* Dec. 1995: 3.